BACKROADS & HIKING TRAILS
THE SANTA CRUZ MOUNTAINS

by Jerry Schad

The Touchstone Press
P.O. Box 81
Beaverton, Oregon 97005

Sprig Lake Trail

area map

1 Huddart Park

2 Sam McDonald Park

3 San Mateo County Memorial Park

4 Portola State Park

5 Butano State Park

6 Henry Cowell Redwoods State Park

7 Castle Rock State Park

8 Big Basin Redwoods State Park

9 Forest of Nisene Marks State Park

10 Uvas Canyon Park

11 Mount Madonna Park

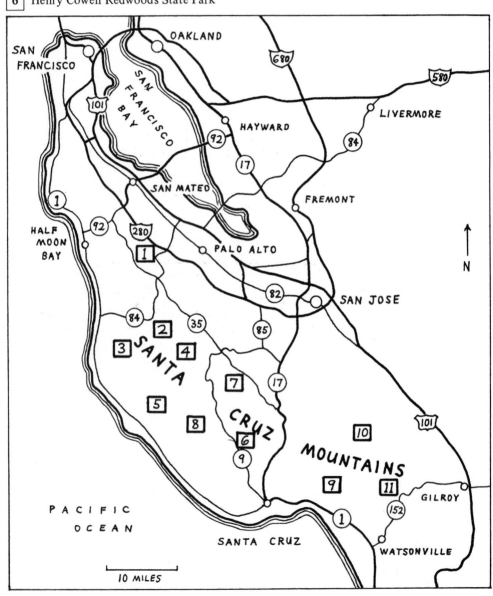

contents

DISCOVERING THE SANTA CRUZ MOUNTAINS

"The innumerable ridges and spurs of the Santa Cruz Range are inter- sected and furrowed by gorges, can- yons, and narrow valleys, trending for the most part seaward, the sides of which are set with forests of pine, redwood, madrone, and other forest trees, the redwoods in many cases having attained gigantic growth. These forests merge into picturesque live-oak openings, whose graceful trees, draped with gray moss, beautify the softer curves of the foot-hills that form the outposts of the main range, and thus seem to guard the exit into the open country of many sparkling streams, which find their sources in the moun- tains, through gloomy gorge and sunlit valley to the sea."

This somewhat romantic description ap- peared nearly 80 years ago in *The Resources of California,* an illustrated journal devoted to the settlement and development of the Golden State. It was written at a time when California was still regarded as the state of unlimited opportunity.

But times have changed. In the interim Northern California has experienced its most profound period of growth: a population expansion originating at San Francisco and neighboring cities that quickly enveloped the shores of the Bay and literally exploded outward to the foothills of the coastal mountain ranges. Here at the mountain barriers, the onrush of urbanization was finally arrested. And to a large degree, the above characterization of the Santa Cruz Mountains — a range whose wooded summits are in view of millions on a clear day — still remains valid today.

In the Santa Cruz Mountains, one can still stand in awe beneath trees of seemingly impossible height that first took root more than a thousand years ago. He can ex- perience the muffled silence and noontime darkness of a hidden canyon. Beside a murmuring stream, he can walk among lacy ferns and lift his eyes to the shimmering of a thousand leaves. The Santa Cruz Mountains — a haven for campers, hikers, birdwatchers, nature lovers.

A well-developed system of roads around the perimeter of the mountains allows quick, easy access from all parts of the San Fran- cisco Bay and Central Coast areas. Santa Cruz, San Jose and the Peninsula cities lie at the base of the range.

Geographically, the Santa Cruz Range forms the backbone of the San Francisco Peninsula. From the hills of San Francisco itself, the main ridge runs southeast, grad- ually rising in elevation to about 3,000 feet before dropping to the Pajaro River near Watsonville. A secondary ridge to the east culminates in a 3,806-foot promontory known as "Loma Prieta" south of San Jose. The principal streams — the San Lorenzo River, and San Gregorio, Pescadero and Soquel Creeks — flow westward to south- ward off the main ridge into the Pacific Ocean. Rainfall is generally abundant. Up to 60 inches of precipitation drenches the area in the period between November and March, supporting a lush growth of vegetation; in the dry summer months, nocturnal fogs often extend well inland keeping the lower elevations cool and moist. Temperatures usually are mild year round with mean lows above freezing in the winter, and mean highs in the 70's during the summer.

The lower elevations are dominated by the coast redwood (Sequoia sempervirens), tallest tree species in the world, and symbol of conservation efforts throughout the state. Upper elevations are covered by mixed forests of pine, fir and deciduous trees, or by grassland and chaparral. Much acreage is tied up in publicly-owned parks, forests and watersheds; the remainder consists of pri- vately-owned parcels that are carefully managed and regulated.

The Santa Cruz Mountains have seen a long and colorful history of logging and related industry. Thanks to the early efforts of citizen groups, many magnificent stands of virgin redwood forest have been preserved in their natural state for the benefit of the present and future generations. This tradition continues today through organizations such as the Sempervirens Fund, the Santa Cruz Mountain Trail Association, and Save-the-Redwoods League.

It is easy to escape to the Santa Cruz Mountains from the cities below by automobile. If you have never explored here, take a drive on "Skyline Boulevard" (California Highway 35), a scenic road following the main ridge overlooking San Francisco Bay and the Pacific Ocean. Numerous other highways cross the range transversely, but only one approaches freeway standards — California 17 between San Jose and Santa Cruz.

Sunday drivers and bicyclists will find the area much to their liking. Meandering back roads are found everywhere. For exploration on wheels, I have included in this book maps and descriptions of eleven trips on back roads that generally serve as alternates to the busy state highways. With one exception (a portion of Mount Madonna Road), these lesser-traveled routes are paved. None is a dead-end. You may easily incorporate these trips into longer loop tours via state highways, or use them as substitute routes to a destination.

Steep grades and unposted sharp turns are common on many of the back roads. Drivers should sound the horn when approaching blind curves. All major and minor roads in the Santa Cruz Mountains are suitable for bicycle travel except Highway 17 (legal in places but extremely dangerous). Bicyclists, however, should recognize that flat ground is the exception: a ten-speed bicycle and moderately-good physical condition are prerequisites for cycling in this area. Speeding motorcycles and sports cars are an occasional hazard.

To fully appreciate the natural environment of the Santa Cruz Mountains, you must leave the road and walk amid the silent forests or climb the open ridges overlooking ocean or bay. In the second half of this book you will find a selected list of 27 hiking trips, ranging in difficulty from easy one-half mile walks to all-day jaunts across ridge and canyon. All trails are within park boundaries, and the majority are suitable for every member of the family. Hiking trips are arranged according to state or county park, accompanied by a brief description and trail map for each park.

Any time of year is a good time to go hiking in the Santa Cruz Mountains, though it would be wise to wear sturdy boots and raingear (or take an umbrella) during the wet winter season. Rattlesnakes are uncommon on most trails, but sighted occasionally in rocky or brushy areas. Poison oak is a very real hazard — learn to recognize it.

I have not included some of the more ambitious trails, such as the Skyline to the Sea Trail. These are more suited for backpacking than day-hiking, and are adequately covered in other publications. Trail camps may be reserved in several of the larger parks — Portola, Butano, Big Basin, Castle Rock and Nisene Marks State Parks. Refer to page 77 for a list of addresses.

It is my hope that this introduction to the Santa Cruz Mountains will serve as an invitation to discovery. Take a reprieve from the pressures of urban living and come up for a day, weekend or longer. Experience the grandeur of the mountains and uncover their hidden secrets. It will be a rewarding adventure for you, as it has been for me.

Old lime kiln

Redwood Grove

BACKROADS

KINGS MOUNTAIN ROAD – TUNITAS CREEK ROAD

The starting point of this backroad trek is the town of Woodside, a bedroom community overlooking Redwood City and the south end of San Francisco Bay. Exit Interstate 280 at Woodside Road (Highway 84), midway between San Francisco and San Jose. Drive 1.5 miles west, past the business district of Woodside, to Kings Mountain Road on the right.

Here you begin the 14-mile stretch of rambling, twisting roads that span the mountain barrier to the Pacific Ocean. Although paved, they are really only slightly-improved versions of original logging supply roads built in the last century. Here, as elsewhere in the Santa Cruz Mountains, the scars of the lumber industry have healed, and time has softened the contours of once-denuded slopes in a green mantle of vigorous second-growth redwoods.

The demand for lumber to build San Francisco during the Gold Rush years of the 1850's resulted in early logging of the Woodside area. No fewer than 15 sawmills were in operation here until about 1865, when timber on the east side of the mountain was nearly depleted. The historic Woodside Store, located 0.7 mile up Kings Mountain Road from Highway 84, was the focal point of activity in these early days. "Old Doc Tripp" (Dr. Robert O. Tripp) left his profession as a dentist in San Francisco to open the store in 1851. The building now standing dates from 1854, and is a public museum.

Kings Mountain Road, originally the Summit Springs Turnpike, was built as a toll road in 1870 to facilitate travel to new logging areas on the upper slopes of the mountain. Today the road continues up through Huddart Park to the summit at Skyline Boulevard. At the top, go straight across to Tunitas Creek Road, which will take you to the ocean.

Young redwoods flanking Tunitas Creek Road stand from streamside to summit as far as the eye can see, crowding together in competition for sunlight. Not a single human habitation is seen for miles until a few hideway cabins and ranch structures appear near the coast.

Tunitas is a nearly non-existent community at Highway 1 along the coast. Tunitas Beach, nearby, was a transfer point for the short-lived and never-completed Ocean Shore Railroad between San Francisco and Santa Cruz. In the years before the railroad's demise in 1920, this was the end of the line for the northern segment of track. Passengers from San Francisco boarded a Stanley Steamer for a bumpy ride south to Swanton, then resumed their journey on rails to Santa Cruz.

SAN GREGORIO TO LA HONDA – THE LONG WAY

A remnant for the "good old days" still exists in San Mateo County. Population spillover from the Bay Area has yet to intrude upon the forgotten coastside quarter of the county south of Half Moon Bay. You need only travel the lonely roads to towns such as San Gregorio and Pescadero to convince yourself of that. The unhurried traveler will enjoy this 23-mile roundabout route from San Gregorio near the coast to La Honda in the heart of the redwood country.

San Gregorio, a small hamlet off Highway 1 about 40 miles south of San Francisco, is a curious mix of neat farmhouses and tumble-down cottages and barns. Peterson and Alsford's General Store in the middle of town is the antithesis of the modern shopping center. You name it, and you'll probably find it here – all under one small roof. Next door is the tiny San Gregorio Post Office.

San Gregorio was a popular resort at the turn of the century before the redwoods were logged out. Look behind the gas station on the corner to see a well-preserved old hotel building and water tower, dating from 1886.

From San Gregorio, head south on Stage Road into the grass and brush-covered hillsides overlooking the ocean. Century-old eucalyptus trees line the road at intervals,

Tunitas Beach

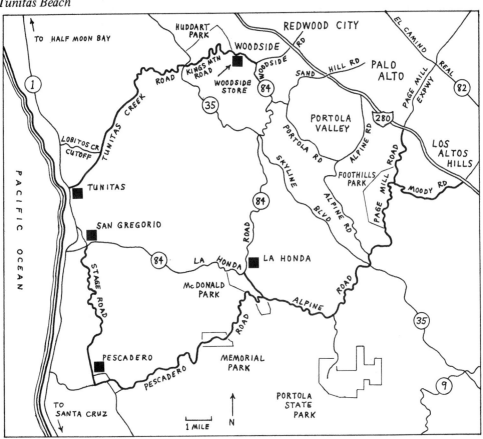

arching overhead at one point to form an arcade. Originally introduced from Australia, the fast-growing eucalyptus were once erroneously thought to have a potential use as lumber. Aside from the practical use today as windbreaks, the eucalyptus adorns many a hillside that would be barren otherwise.

After many ups and downs, Stage Road emerges upon the gentle farmland of Pescadero. Dominating the skyline before you reach the town itself is the white steeple of the New England-style Pescadero Community Church, built in 1868. The white wood siding of the church was carefully crafted to simulate stone. Drive up North Street for a look at the rows of brightly-colored old frame houses lining the street. Saint Anthony's Church, on the left, is another architectural gem, built in 1870.

Pescadero is an agricultural community of about a thousand inhabitants, most of Portuguese descent. The area was first settled in the 1850's, and like San Gregorio, became a popular resort for San Franciscans in the late 1800's.

Every year, on the weekend before Pentecost (the fifth Sunday after Easter), Pescadero residents host a "Chamarita," a Portuguese celebration commemorating deliverance from natural disasters and starvation on the Azores hundreds of years ago. The festival includes a parade, dances and a free barbeque.

To continue the trip, follow Pescadero Road eastward along the banks of Pescadero Creek. The dairyland and farming (mostly artichokes and brussels sprouts) along the creek soon becomes constricted to a narrow strip as redwoods close in overhead. At San Mateo County Memorial Park, the road leaves the creek and begins a winding ascent. A spectacular view to the west unfolds as the road enters a clearing on the steep slopes near the top of the ridge. Descending, you pass Sam McDonald Park and re-enter the redwood forest.

Pescadero Road ends at Highway 84, not far from the small resort community of La Honda. From here you might wish to return to San Gregorio — or continue eastward up to Skyline Boulevard.

PAGE MILL ROAD — ALPINE ROAD

Numerous turns — some posted at 10 mph — demand the constant attention of even slow drivers on this route, which runs from Palo Alto, up and over Skyline Ridge, to the redwood country near La Honda. Highly scenic throughout, it offers unmatched panoramas of both San Francisco Bay and the Pacific Ocean from altitudes of over 2,000 feet.

You may begin at the Page Mill Road interchange on Interstate 280, or use Moody Road as a connector from I-280 at Los Altos Hills. Either way, it's 8½ miles of uphill to the summit at Skyline Road (Highway 35). Low gear may be required at times.

Page Mill Road has become a favorite — though very challenging — road for Bay Area bicyclists. Considerable strength is required to turn even the "alpine" gears of modern ten-speeds when a cyclist is climbing grades exceeding 10 percent. Likewise, skill in handling comes into play when a cyclist negotiates the corkscrew descents back to the lowlands.

Foothills Park, a private park reserved for Palo Alto citizens, is passed on the right about five miles up from Interstate 280. When you reach the stop sign at Skyline Boulevard, at the top of the hill, continue straight across on Alpine Road.

The next seven miles offer an interesting study in contrasts — the vegetation depending upon the elevation and the availability of water. Open grasslands with airy views dominate the sunny ridge tops that attend you as far as the turnoff for Portola State Park (remain on Alpine Road at this intersection). Then there comes a quick descent through oak and madrone — often through a fog layer — into a thick blanket of redwoods enshrouding Alpine Creek. A few cabins, forever in shade, nestle among the gigantic trunks along the banks of the creek. Alpine Road ends here at Pescardero Road, just a short distance from Sam McDonald Park and a little more than one mile from La Honda.

Eucalyptus arcade – Stage Road

SWANTON ROAD

Few people speeding along the coast highway between San Francisco and Santa Cruz notice the small green sign indicating Swanton Road. Yet here is an ideal diversion for those weary of coastside scenery. At the expense of only a few extra minutes, travelers on Highway 1 can enjoy a peaceful ride through a canyon grown thick with oak, bay and redwood trees, and return again to the coast to resume their trip.

Travelers northbound out of Santa Cruz will reach the southern end of this inland loop about two miles beyond Davenport. Leaving Highway 1, the road winds by weatherbeaten old farm houses and passes behind a low range of hills hiding the coastline. The valley narrows, and suddenly you're in the redwoods. The small hamlet of Swanton slumbers peacefully here — just an old schoolhouse and a few old homes. Eighty years ago, this was a busy canyon. Promoter Fred Swanton organized the Big Creek Light & Power Company here in 1896, and soon was furnishing electricity to Santa Cruz, Watsonville and Ben Lomond via transmission lines. Wood-fired steam generators were used at first; later hydro-power was utilized. Swanton's power plant was maintained up until 1948, when a forest fire caused considerable damage.

The Swanton area has become a haven for independent artisans and craftsmen. Open on weekends and holidays during most of the year are the rustic homes of Scott Creek Pottery and Big Creek Pottery. Look for them on the inland side of Swanton Road.

Immediately beyond the redwood buildings of Big Creek Pottery, Swanton Road takes a nosedive toward the coast, where it rejoins Highway 1. Views of the Pacific Ocean are magnificent on the way down — if possible, come here to watch the sunset on a clear day.

FELTON TO DAVENPORT

Winding ascents and descents are the rule on this 14-mile trek across the mountains from Felton to the ocean. However, many opportunities are available to gape at the idyllic scenery along the way, and these are likely to outweigh any misgivings about carsickness. Roads in this area are uncrowded, typically, allowing you a leisurely pace to look around.

Felton is a picturesque mountain community located along the San Lorenzo River a few miles north of Santa Cruz. Don't miss the covered bridge over the San Lorenzo built in 1892. You'll discover it about 500 feet south of the main river crossing (Mt. Hermon Road) near the center of town. The covered bridge is not open to automobile traffic, but pedestrians and equestrians use it regularly.

To begin the trip, drive west on Bennett Street from the traffic signal in the middle of Felton. Bennett becomes Felton-Empire Road and begins twisting up the redwood-shaded flanks of Ben Lomond Mountain. Much of the area to the right was recently acquired as park land by the State of California. On the left side of the road, about two miles from Felton, a clear running stream has been tapped to provide drinking water for passersby. The quality of this water is renowned among both natives and visitors.

Cross Empire Grade at the top of the mountain and continue westward on Ice Cream Grade. Here is a classic example of a paved road evolved from a wagon track. Little of the natural topography was disturbed here, in contrast to modern methods of road construction. The road dips in and out of a deeply-shaded ravine and emerges upon a rolling tableland and ranching area known as Bonny Doon.

Turn right at Pine Flat Road, proceed 0.2 mile north to Bonny Doon Road, then make a left turn. This part was once named "Ocean View Avenue," and if you're lucky you might catch a glimpse of the blue arc of the Pacific in the distance. Bonny Doon Road takes you into the business district of Bonny Doon, consisting of nothing more than a saloon. Turn right here and begin a three-mile descent to Highway 1 and the coast.

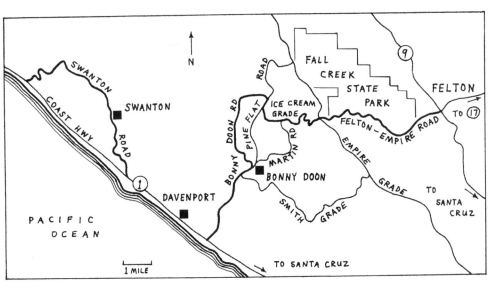

As you descend, you'll notice that the rolling meadows and forests of Bonny Doon thin out, and the ground cover becomes a tough mixture of chaparral. Sand and gravel quarries nearby provide the raw materials for the big cement plant at Davenport. The plant has recently taken measures to curb emissions of cement dust from its giant smokestack, and Davenport today is a town emerging from a dingy past into a bright future. From the intersection of Highway 1 and Bonny Doon Road, Davenport is one mile to the north and Santa Cruz is ten miles to the south.

BEAR CREEK ROAD

Bear Creek Road consists of 14 miles of scenic, slow-speed blacktop between Highway 17 at Lexington Reservoir and Highway 9 at Boulder Creek. Though it is sometimes used by Santa Cruz- or San Jose-bound motorists as a bypass around summer traffic on Highway 17, non-goal oriented tourists will enjoy this route for its own value.

Southbound travelers on 17 may make a right turn onto Bear Creek Road about two miles south of Los Gatos. The road climbs stiffly past vineyards and country estates, and winds through pockets of oak and redwood forest before reaching the summit ridge of the Santa Cruz Mountains. In two miles you'll see a fishing pond and buildings belonging to Daybreak, a private experimental school. From 1934 to 1967 Alma College, a Jesuit school of theology, occupied this campus. California Governor Jerry Brown is perhaps this seminary's most famous former student. In another mile you'll come to the stately home of Presentation College; formerly it was the Montezuma School for Boys.

At the top of the grade, Summit Road joins from the left. Bear right at this intersection; a left would return you to Highway 17. In another mile, Skyline Boulevard branches to the right — the beginning of the famous ridge-top route to San Francisco. Keep left at this intersection to remain on Bear Creek Road.

Ten miles farther and 1,700 feet below is the small, but growing community of Boulder Creek, one of several such towns along the San Lorenzo River. From here you may turn south on Highway 9 to Felton and Santa Cruz, north on Highway 9 back to the Santa Clara Valley, or west on Highway 236 toward Big Basin.

THE OLD SANTA CRUZ HIGHWAY

For thousands of years, Costanoan Indians labored on foot over the mountain barrier separating the Santa Clara Valley from the coast. With the coming of the white man, and particularly with the influx of settlers during the Gold Rush, the mountains quickly yielded to the horse and buggy. A toll road, the Santa Cruz Turnpike, was completed in 1858, making it possible to travel between the cities of Santa Cruz and Santa Clara in as little as five hours.

By 1880, a narrow-gauge railroad — the "Picnic Line" — spanned the Santa Cruz Mountains. Valley residents boarded the train at Los Gatos bound for Santa Cruz, and enjoyed a lunch stop enroute amid the giant redwoods along San Lorenzo River.

The earthquake of 1906 damaged the Picnic Line extensively, but reconstruction followed during the next three years, and included a conversion to standard-gauge. Today's long-time local residents look back fondly upon the era of the "Suntan Special," an era that ended in 1940.

In 1916, a practical alternative to rail transportation was inaugurated with the completion of a state auto road across the mountains. Even after concrete paving in 1919, it was scarcely wide enough to accommodate the passage of two automobiles, let alone wider vehicles. Today a "new" highway (California 17), built just prior to World War II and improved several times since, carries motorists quickly and efficiently across the summits.

Much of the "Old Santa Cruz Highway" is still in existence thanks to improvements and maintenance by the Santa Clara and Santa Cruz County highway departments. Both the old and the new routes accomplish

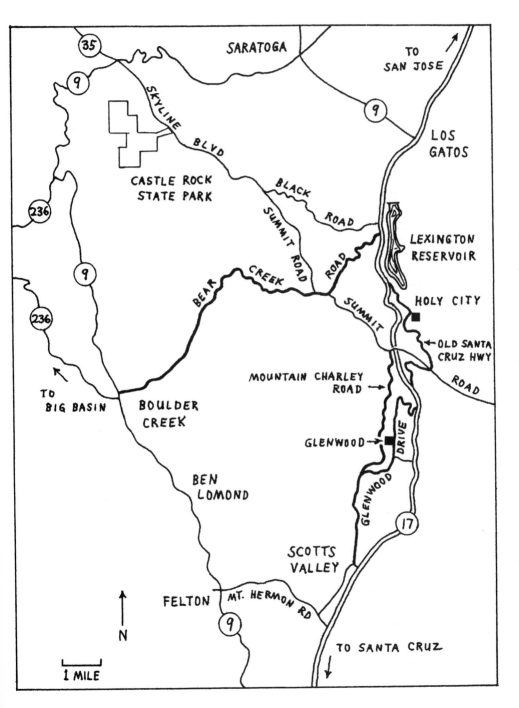

the same end, but only the old highway offers a slow-paced look at the redwood forest and the historical points of interest along this important transportation corridor.

To trace the existent remnants of the old highway (assuming you are a motorist southbound on Highway 17 from San Jose), drive through Los Gatos and begin the first ascent into the mountains. On the left, below Lexington Dam, is a canyon that contains a disconnected portion of the old road. The narrow concrete ribbon continues beneath the impounded waters of Lexington Reservoir, passing near the submerged townsites of Alma and Lexington (former stops along the railroad line). You can reach the first accessible portion of the original route at the south end of the reservoir. Turn left at the sign on Highway 17 reading "Old Santa Cruz Highway" to reach it.

At about 1½ miles from the turnoff at Highway 17 you enter Moody Gulch and cross a great slide. The San Andreas Rift Zone passes through this area in a northwest to southeast direction. Nearby, in the gulch, is the site of an 1873 oil discovery — a rare occurrence in Northern California. As late as 1922, oil from a producing well here was sold in San Jose.

In another mile you'll come to the semi-ghost town of Holy City. In 1919, the Rev. William E. Riker, self-styled religious leader and founder of the "Perfect Christian Divine Way," moved his small colony of followers from San Francisco to his version of New Jerusalem in the Santa Cruz Mountains. Throughout the twenties and thirties, Holy City's business establishments thrived on the tourist trade provided by the highway. Attractions included alcoholic soda pop, religious peep shows, a mystery exhibit, observatory, and zoo. Riker's "Headquarters for the World's Perfect Government" offered $25,000 to anyone who could detect a flaw in his system. Little remained of Holy City after a fire in 1959. Riker's house and a few other buildings still stand, along with a few new ones, but members of his colony have long since dispersed.

A monument at Patchen, one mile past Holy City, describes some additional area

history. Continue the winding ascent on Old Santa Cruz Highway to Summit Road, then cross over to Woodwardia Highway — the quietest and least disturbed section of old highway. After two miles you're back at Highway 17. At this point you must make a left turn onto the busy lanes and proceed one-half mile south to where Glenwood Drive (old Glenwood Highway) begins abruptly on the right. Exercise extreme caution on this stretch, as both intersections are dangerous.

Back on the narrow concrete ribbon again, you can relax and appreciate the next three miles as you descend through a redwood hollow to the site of Glenwood and its famous resort hotel. A monument on the right side of the road gives details of the area's history.

On the west side of the road, 500 feet north of the Glenwood monument, is the west entrance to the longest of six tunnels on the San Jose—Santa Cruz railroad line. This one, more than one-mile long, caved in during the 1906 earthquake, and after reconstruction became part of the Suntan Special. The tunnel entrance is now sealed, and the old railroad bed is difficult to trace after nearly 40 years.

The old highway route continues along Glenwood Drive to Scotts Valley, where it disappears under the pavement of old Highway 17 (Scotts Valley Road) and the newer freeway to Santa Cruz. The detour from Lexington Reservoir to Scotts Valley has added five additional miles to your odometer and an hour or more to your trip to Santa Cruz — but wasn't it worth it?

MOUNTAIN CHARLEY ROAD

The Spaniards and Indians called him "Mountain Charley," but he was known also by more colorful names such as "Silver Skull Charley" and "Hair-Brain Charley," in reference to his famous encounter with a grizzly bear. Who was he?

Born in Ireland in 1812, Charles Henry McKiernan worked his way by ship to San Francisco in 1848, and soon became the first to settle on the summit of the Santa Cruz

Vineyards along Bear Creek Road

Pond at Daybreak School

Mountains between San Jose and Santa Cruz. He tried raising sheep, but was plagued with constant attacks from mountain lions and grizzly bear. To supplement his income, he hunted deer for the San Francisco market. On one of these hunts, an old she-bear with cubs attacked, tearing a gaping hole in Charley's skull and leaving him blind in one eye. Fortunately, help arrived and Charley was taken to his cabin where a doctor closed the wound in his head with a plate made by hammering out a Mexican silver dollar. Later, after Charley complained of severe headaches, a Redwood City doctor reopened the old wound and removed a wad of hair that was lodged underneath the silver plate — hence the above nicknames!

In later years Charley constructed a road across his property as part of the Santa Cruz Turnpike. Except for a modern coating of blacktop and the absence of a toll, the road is little changed today and still bears the name of its builder.

A five-mile segment of Mountain Charley Road may be driven slowly (speed limit: 20 mph) as an alternate to busy Highway 17. Southbound motorists can exit at the Summit Road interchange and pick up the old toll road about 200 yards west of Highway 17.

The road is typical of horse and wagon trails of that era — with short, steep climbs and long, flat runs where the teams could rest. At one mile from Summit Road is a log house with an historical marker out front. The house was built by Charles McKiernan's nephew in the early 1900's; Charley's cabin site lies nearby.

At the bottom of the grade, five miles from Summit Road, Mountain Charley Road merges with Glenwood Drive. From here you can continue an additional three miles to Scotts Valley and a return to Highway 17 toward Santa Cruz.

SUMMIT ROAD
TO CORRALITOS

Summit Road, a lesser-known extension of the famous Skyline Boulevard, continues southward along the crest of the Santa Cruz Mountains for some miles into pastoral farmland presided over by noble Loma Prieta, the highest mountain of the Santa Cruz range (3,806 feet). A scenic parkway, under consideration for many years, would extend the summit route even farther over existing primitive roads to Highway 152 at Mt. Madonna Park. Today, however, the south end of Summit Road is linked only to an obscure paved road which provides a scenic short-cut between the Santa Clara Valley and the Watsonville area of southern Santa Cruz County.

Go first to the Highway 17/Summit Road interchange, located midway between San Jose and Santa Cruz, at the crest of the hill. (You may also reach this point by way of Skyline Boulevard.)

In the first mile, as you travel southeast from Highway 17, you'll notice flat-topped Loma Prieta directly ahead. Impenetrable thickets of chaparral clothe the mountain's flanks, and are responsible for its name, translated as "dark mountain."

The sunny hillsides and ridges along Summit Road are an excellent habitat for vines and fruit trees. A few orchards still are producing — others, sad to say, are giving way to subdivisions. At about five miles from Highway 17, you'll come to the tiny communities of Highland and Skyland. Highland was here first, so the story goes; but, residents of the newer community were not to be outdone by its lofty-sounding neighbor.

Here, Summit Road narrows, becomes Highland Way, and begins a gradual descent from the crest of the mountains. Soquel Creek cut the deep, V-shaped gorge below you; beyond is a large tract of undeveloped land, part of the Forest of Nisene Marks State Park. A small slice of coastline appears ahead, weather permitting.

About 12 miles from Highway 17, the road name changes again — to Eureka Canyon Road — and the road now straddles the San Andreas Fault for three miles before making an abrupt turn westward. Surface scars from the fault are difficult to detect here, because of the heavy growth of redwoods.

Finally, at 21 miles, you arrive at Corralitos, a mere crossroads today, but a busy place in the 1860's. In its prime, the town had 20 houses, two stores, a wagon and blacksmith shop, a flour mill, a schoolhouse and three sawmills.

From Corralitos, a network of country roads branches out to all parts of the beautiful apple-growing region around Watsonville. You may travel south on Corralitos Road, then east on Freedom Boulevard to reach Watsonville; or take Hames Road and Freedom Boulevard west toward Highway 1 to reach Santa Cruz.

OVER THE HILL ON
MOUNT MADONNA ROAD

Mount Madonna Road — or "Old Watsonville Road" — preceded the present Hecker Pass Highway (California 152) across the mountains between Gilroy and Watsonville. Evolved from an early toll road, it has served generations of early travelers, and is still in limited use today. In deference to the needs of equestrians, a 1½-mile steep section has been left unpaved; therefore this trip should not be taken during periods of wet weather.

If you are traveling this route from east to west (Gilroy to Watsonville), take Highway 152 west from Gilroy to Watsonville Road, then proceed one mile north to Redwood Retreat Road. A number of small, independent wineries cluster in this part of the Santa Clara Valley; you will notice an abundance of vineyards set upon the gentle foothills along the edge of the valley. Orchards and grazing land accompany the vines as you gain elevation, and live oaks form a leafy canopy at one point along Redwood Retreat Road.

At three miles from Watsonville Road, Mount Madonna Road leaves Redwood Retreat Road to begin a steep ascent of the

Old shack near Mount Madonna Road

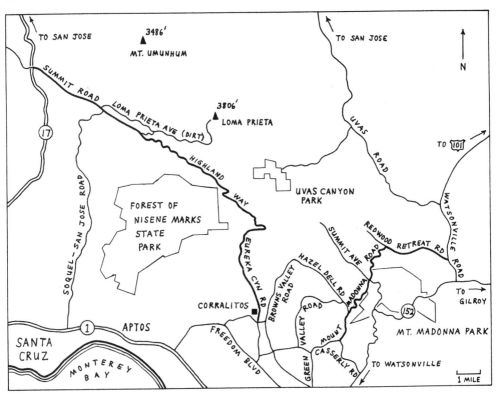

west side of the mountain. (The remainder of Redwood Retreat Road is a short spur leading to Robert Louis Stevenson's turn-of-the-century summer home — his favorite retreat in the redwoods.) Driving uphill on Mount Madonna Road, you'll soon encounter the aforementioned unpaved section. Pavement resumes at the intersection of Summit Avenue on the western edge of Mount Madonna Park, a point marking the 1,710-foot crest of the old toll road. Immediately you begin a winding descent toward the coastal plain, with glimpses of the verdant Pajaro Valley, replete with apple blossoms in springtime, below you. At the bottom of the grade, turn left (remaining on Mount Madonna Road) to return to Highway 152. You may either head west on Hwy 152 back to Gilroy, or east to reach Watsonville and the Coast Highway.

A LOOP THROUGH NEW ALMADEN

New Almaden lies only about two miles from the outlying suburban sprawl of south San Jose, yet a more peaceful spot would be difficult to find anywhere. This quiet village, tucked amid the southeastern spurs of the Santa Cruz Mountains, belies its past history, for New Almaden has played an important part in early California's development. The first mining operations in the state were believed to have taken place here in 1824, following the discovery of large deposits of cinnabar, a mercury-bearing mineral, on the nearby hillsides.

The mining community which was christened here in 1847 lived up to its namesake, the fabulously rich quicksilver mine of Almaden, Spain. Mercury is the chief reduction agent for extraction of gold from ore, and production boomed at New Almaden in the latter days of California's Gold Rush. New Almaden became the richest quicksilver mine in North America — over one million flasks of quicksilver valued in excess of $50,000,000 were eventually produced. Mining activity has only recently ended here, after more than a century of continuous activity.

Since two routes connect New Almaden with San Jose, it's convenient to make this excursion a loop trip. To get there in a hurry, drive south on Almaden Expressway through the Almaden Valley. Beyond the last of the subdivisions the expressway reverts to the original Almaden Road, a two-lane thoroughfare leading directly to New Almaden. The village has changed little in the past two decades, in spite of the southward march of suburbia which now threatens to engulf it. Alamitos Creek trickles unhurriedly through town, and the inhabitants of elderly, but well-kept cottages seem to relish the serenity of their little hideway in the mountains.

Weekend visitors stop at the New Almaden Museum to view relics of the mining days, or pay a visit to the famous hacienda — Casa Grande. General Halleck, manager of the mine in its early days, designed this stately 27-room building as his personal operations headquarters. Construction began in 1852. By the late 1880's the Casa Grande had become a luxury resort hotel for San Francisco society. It remains in use as a resort even today.

Hundreds of acres of old mining property

Stellers jay

26

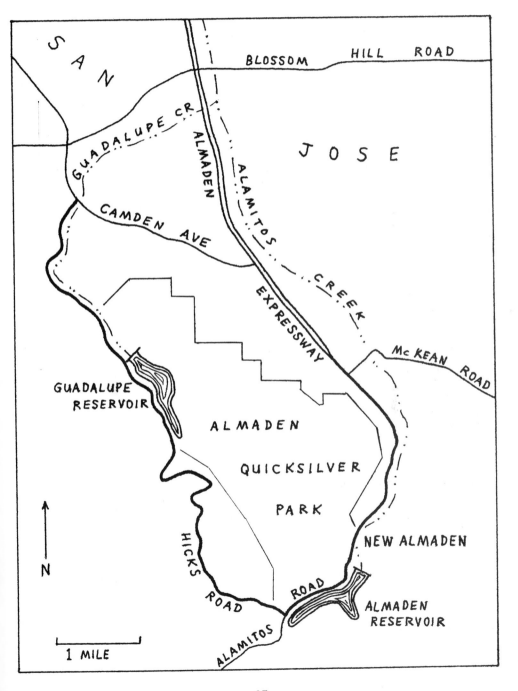

SAN

JOSE

BLOSSOM HILL ROAD

GUADALUPE CR.

ALMADEN

ALAMITOS CREEK

CAMDEN AVE

EXPRESSWAY

Mc KEAN ROAD

GUADALUPE
RESERVOIR

ALMADEN

QUICKSILVER

PARK

NEW ALMADEN

N

HICKS ROAD

ALMADEN
RESERVOIR

ALAMITOS ROAD

1 MILE

in the honeycombed hills above town have recently been purchased by Santa Clara County for use as a regional park. The new bridle paths in the park are a first step toward eventual development.

On the return to San Jose, the back way, you'll pass two of the eleven Water Conservation District reservoirs in Santa Clara County. During summer dry periods, water impounded behind Almaden and Guadalupe Dams is released downstream to feed "percolation ponds" in the valley below. Slow seepage of water through the porous strata below the percolation ponds replenishes the valley's subterranean water table. Most of Santa Clara County's water supply is dependent upon wells which tap this storehouse of underground water.

Hicks Road, linking the two reservoirs, climbs to a saddle at an elevation of 1,400 feet, affording a spectacular view of the chaparral-clad Loma Prieta, the "Dark Mountain." Low gear may be necessary to negotiate the grades approaching 15 percent on either side of the summit. The continuation of Hicks Road below Guadalupe Reservoir connects with Camden Avenue in San Jose.

Along Castle Rock Trail

HIKING TRAILS

HUDDART PARK

San Mateo County's Huddart Park is one of several similar-sized county parks in the Santa Cruz Mountains. It is located on the east slope of the range near Woodside, along Kings Mountain Road. In addition to an extensive network of interconnecting riding and hiking trails, the park has a more than usual share of recreational facilities. These include picnicking sites, a campground (open in summer), a horse ring, a playground, and an archery range.

Elevations within the 973 acres range from 500 feet to more than 2,000 feet at the western boundary along Skyline Boulevard. Because dissimilar climatic conditions exist along the slope, a great variety of life zones are found here. In the redwood forest along the streambeds, sword ferns and redwood sorrel furnish a cool and moist environment for banana slugs and salamanders. Frequently adjacent to the redwood belts are the hot and dry chaparral areas, where dense thickets of manzanita, chamise, chaparral pea and yerba santa provide sufficient cover for jackrabbits, chipmunks, lizards and quail.

The upper elevations of the park are primarily mixed evergreen forest, with tan-oak (tanbark oak), madrone, California bay, coast live oak and Douglas fir dominant. Shrubs found beneath these trees include wild lilac, monkey flower, toyon, wood rose and poison oak, not to mention the annual wildflowers. Wildlife includes Columbian black-tailed deer, raccoons and gray squirrels. Stellers jays, acorn woodpeckers and chickadees are the birds most often seen or heard.

Huddart Park is a microcosm of the many diverse environments of the Santa Cruz Mountains. A good way to familiarize yourself with these environments is to walk the Chickadee Nature Trail described below. No account of the other 14 miles of trail in the outlying parts of the park will be given here. These are equestrian trails for the most part, and due to the steep topography, they are generally difficult for hikers.

Gray squirrel

Chickadee Nature Trail

Approximate distance: 0.7 mile round trip
Elevation at trailhead: 800 feet
Low point: 730 feet
High point: 890 feet

This is a self-guiding nature trail with lettered marker posts, so pick up a copy of the Chickadee Nature Trail Guide at the entrance station before you begin the hike. The trail begins at the first parking lot to the right on the entrance road.

Listen for the clearly enunciated "chick-a-dee-dee-dee" or "dee-dee-dee" sound of the chestnut-backed chickadee among the oaks. A very interesting effect of temperature contrast between differing vegetation areas is mentioned in the guide. During the summer months, a 20° difference in the space of a few yards is not uncommon at one point on the trail. Also of interest are the remains of an eroded "skid road" used by lumbermen a century ago. Oxen and horses were used to drag redwood logs down from the mountains on greased skidways such as this to loading areas below. From there they were taken by wagon to the mills at Redwood City.

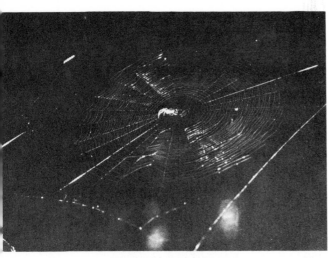

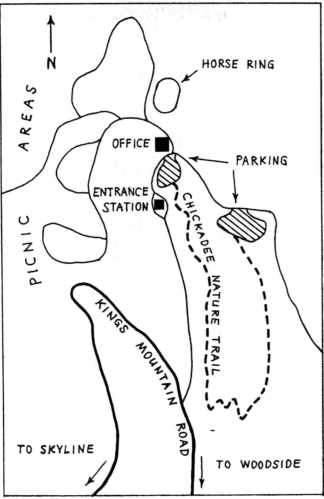

N

HORSE RING

PICNIC AREAS

OFFICE

PARKING

ENTRANCE STATION

CHICKADEE NATURE TRAIL

KINGS MOUNTAIN ROAD

TO SKYLINE

TO WOODSIDE

SAM McDONALD PARK

Steep Sam McDonald County Park is located on Pescadero Road about three miles south of La Honda. Automobiles and other motor vehicles are not permitted in the interior of the park, but may be parked in the office area just off Pescadero Road. Three flat, cleared areas with barbeque pits, picnic tables and restrooms in the north-western half of the park are available for picnicking. Overnight camping is limited to organized groups such as Boy and Girl Scouts. Both first- and second-growth red-woods are found on the steep slopes here, a result of selective logging procedures early in the century.

A new addition to the southeastern por-tion of Sam McDonald Park now enables a hiker to walk into the recently acquired Pescadero Creek Park without crossing pri-vate land. Containing an enormous 6,000 acres of redwood forest, Pescadero Creek Park is presently open for day hiking. An interconnecting system of fire roads exists here, linking together the trails of Sam McDonald Park, Memorial Park and Portola State Park. If you wish to hike through Pescadero Creek Park, consult with the ranger at Sam McDonald Park concerning the details. The next decade will see the development of camping facilities in Pes-cadero Creek park, and the realization of a compreshensive trail system for all four parks.

McDonald Trail

Approximate distance: 2.5 miles round trip on northwestern loop
1.5 miles round trip on southeastern loop
Elevation at park headquarters: 640 feet
High point (southeastern loop): 1,000 feet

The McDonald Trail is divided into two parts, both of which originate at the park office. The longer loop rises through a dense redwood and fern forest northwest of the office, while the shorter loop begins on the edge of the parking lot opposite the office and crosses Pescadero Road to the wooded slopes in the southeastern end of the park. The biggest standing redwoods in the park, and the largest stumps, are seen on the southeastern loop. Notches cut for loggers' springboards can be seen on some of the old stumps. Special arrowhead-shaped symbols on the trail markers guide you around both loops of the trail, and from time to time you'll be traveling fire roads that rise and fall with the sloping terrain.

Redwood forest

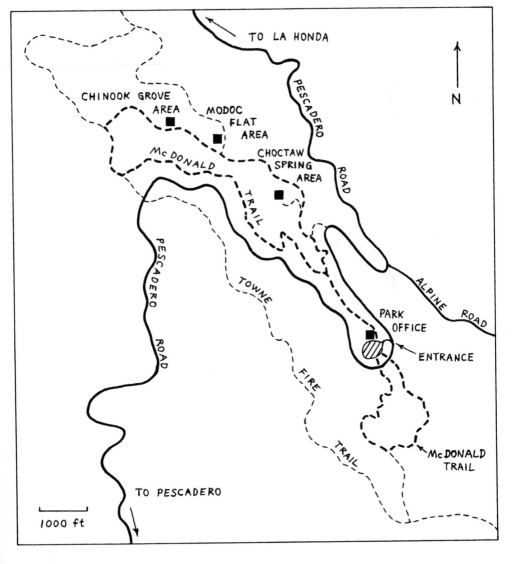

TO LA HONDA

PESCADERO ROAD

N

CHINOOK GROVE AREA

MODOC FLAT AREA

McDONALD

CHOCTAW SPRING AREA

TRAIL

PESCADERO ROAD

TOWNE

ALPINE ROAD

PARK OFFICE

ENTRANCE

FIRE

TRAIL

McDONALD TRAIL

1000 ft

TO PESCADERO

SAN MATEO COUNTY MEMORIAL PARK

Memorial Park was acquired in 1924 and named in memory of the soldiers who died in World War I. Setting aside this land for public use served to protect a small portion of the primeval redwood forest and anticipated the heavy recreational use that is associated with the park today. The park contains about 320 acres situated astride Pescadero Road midway between La Honda and Pescadero. The area south of the road is devoted mostly to automobile-oriented camping and picnicking, with 174 overnight campsites available on a non-reservation basis, picnic tables and barbeque pits for day use, and cleared areas suitable for games and sports. Visitors can also fish for trout or walk the trails along Pescadero Creek. A dammed-up swimming hole and sunny strip of sand along the creek is inviting on warm days. Nature lovers will probably best enjoy the Mount Ellen Trail in the quiet "natural area" north of the road.

Mount Ellen Nature Trail

Approximate distances: 1.0 mile round trip on Nature Trail only
1.8 miles including side trip to Mount Ellen summit
Low point (trailhead): 410 feet
High point (Mount Ellen): 680 feet

First obtain a copy of the Mount Ellen Trail Guide at the entrance to the park, then walk across Pescadero Road to the trailhead. If you have already walked the nature trail at Huddart Park or are familiar with the flora of the east slope of the Santa Cruz Mountains, try making a comparison with the items listed on this trail guide. Common species exist on both sides of the range, but many are different. Memorial Park has a greater amount of rainfall (typically 50 to 60 inches a year) and supports a more luxuriant growth of evergreens because it lies on the ocean-facing slope of the range.

The Nature Trail loop is taken in a counterclockwise direction according to the trail guide. The 0.4 mile-long trail to Mount Ellen intersects the Nature Trail after marker post "K". At the top the view is somewhat obstructed by trees, but nonetheless is pleasing.

Bracken fern

36

Western azalea

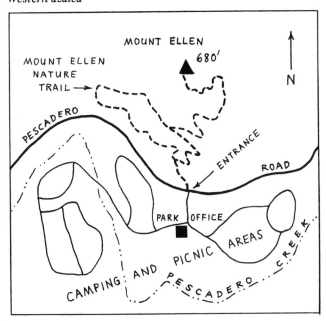

PORTOLA STATE PARK

Measured by crows' flight, Portola State Park is just a few miles from the metropolitan crescent around south San Francisco Bay. By road over Skyline Ridge — maybe twice as far. But when you're there ... it seems a thousand miles from civilization.

Portola is one of the more established redwood parks. Acquired from lumber interests in 1924 by the Islam Shrine (a Masonic organization) for use as a park, it was sold to the State of California in 1945. Timber cutting here, as elsewhere in the Santa Cruz Mountains, was the main industry in the late nineteenth century. Many of the larger trees that were considered imperfect by standards of the time were left standing; clear cutting was unheard of as a lumbering practice in those days. Today the remaining giants, as well as the regenerated growth of smaller trees around the old redwood stumps, are a delight to the visitor.

The major watercourse of the area, Pescadero Creek, meanders through the park, interfaced in places by sheer cliffs. Two tributaries, Peters Creek and Slate Creek, also traverse the park. Oil slicks frequently appear in the slow-moving backwaters of these streams. This is not man-made pollution, but natural seepage from petroleum deposits underground.

To reach Portola from the Bay Area, take any road from the Peninsula up to Skyline Boulevard (Highway 35). The park is seven twisting miles down from Skyline via Alpine Road. A small museum is located at the Visitor Center in the main area of the park. Fifty-two developed family campsites and several picnic areas are nearby, as well as facilities for large groups. The remainder of the park is a natural area, accessible only by hiking trails.

Sequoia Nature Trail

Approximate distance: 0.5 mile round trip
Trail elevation: 400 feet

Starting behind the Visitor Center, the marker posts along this self-guided nature trail point out the common natural features of the environment of the coast redwood. The most impressive item on the list, and certainly the most unusual sight in the park, is the "Shell Tree" at post No. 10. It is theorized that this tree has experienced many successive fires over its lifetime of roughly 2,000 years. Although the heartwood was eventually burned completely out of the trunk, a small amount of sapwood survived each blaze providing a link between the roots and needles. The tree continues to support a healthy crown today, a living testimony to the persistence of the redwood after fire.

The Sequoia Nature Trail crosses Pescadero Creek, which plays host to crayfish and several species of fish including the migratory steelhead trout. You may inquire at the Visitor Center about fishing regulations. During the rainy season, the wooden footbridges across the creek are removed, and it might be necessary to use the permanent bridge upstream near Iverson Cabin to reach the other side.

Shell tree

38

Iverson cabin

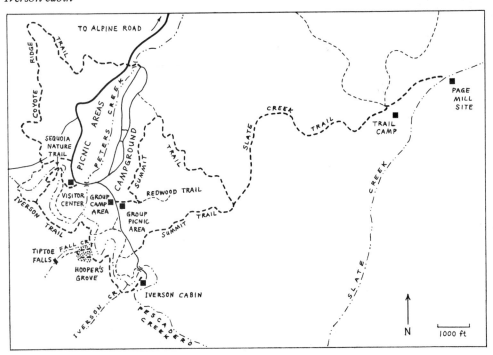

Iverson Trail

Approximate distance: 1.5 miles (1 way)
Low point: 400 feet
High point: 480 feet

Iverson Trail can be reached by an off-shoot of Sequoia Nature Trail on the far side of Pescadero Creek. The trail goes upstream along the creek, but never comes very close to the water's edge. Instead, it meanders along through huckleberry thickets, and on one occasion rises to the top of a high bluff overlooking the creek. Some caution would be in order here if you have small children, since the path has no railings.

A short side-trip up Fall Creek, a small tributary of Pescadero Creek, reveals Tiptoe Falls. Some splendid redwood trees may be seen in the vicinity of Fall Creek, and the best of these are included in a group named Hooper's Grove. Chris Iverson's Cabin, at the end of the trail, was built of redwood by the earliest known settler of the area. Reputedly a Pony Express rider, Iverson came to Pescadero Creek in the 1860's to make a living at splitting shakes. In spite of little maintenance through the years, his home remains standing today. Such is the value of redwood lumber that it can withstand the ravages of time and the elements.

Coyote Ridge Trail

Approximate distance: 1.6 miles (1 way)
Low point (trailhead): 415 feet
High point (Coyote Ridge): 1,010 feet

Here's a trail for hill-climbing enthusiasts. Beginning just north of the Visitor Center at an elevation of 415 feet, it rises to 1,010 feet atop Coyote Ridge, then descends abruptly to the entrance road along Peters Creek. Wear sturdy boots with lug soles on this hike as some sections are quite slippery.

About half-way up you'll see a specimen of poison oak grown far beyond its usual proportions as a small vine or shrub. This one has become the size of a tree, attaching itself to a Douglas fir as if to strangle the tree.

Summit Trail — Slate Creek Trail

Approximate distances: 2.3 miles round trip on Summit Trail only
6.7 miles round trip including Page Mill site
Low point (trailhead): 430 feet
High point (Slate Creek Trail): 1,030 feet

In spite of its length, a hike around Summit Trail, including the side trip on Slate Creek Trail, is not really very difficult. Aside from an easy climb of just under 600 feet to the top of the ridge, and a corresponding drop to complete the Summit Loop, the additional mileage to the Page Mill site is mostly flat and well worth the effort for the scenery alone, if not the exercise.

To find the trailhead starting from the Visitor Center, walk across Peters Creek to the group camp and group picnic areas. From here, take Redwood Trail 0.1 mile east to Summit Trail. Redwood Trail itself continues another 0.2 mile to the tallest tree in the park, a hulking giant with a diameter of 12 feet.

After an initial climb, Summit Trail settles into an easy grade to the top of the ridge. At the sign reading "Slate Creek — 1.7 miles," turn if you wish to continue; if not then straight ahead will complete the loop.

Slate Creek Trail is remarkably flat, even when the terrain becomes precipitous around it. It runs along the south side of the ridge, then crosses over a saddle to the north side, rarely straying from the 1,000-foot contour. The redwoods that were so commonly seen in the early part of the hike make only scattered appearances along the ridge top; instead an exceedingly dense growth of associated types such as tanoak and madrone predominate. A few remains are all that can be found around the old Page lumber mill site at the point where Slate Creek Trail reaches the creek.

The remaining part of Summit Trail crosses over a small chaparral zone with a view of Butano Ridge to the south. The sign here reads "Summit — Elevation 980 feet." Continue downhill to the paved service road that leads back to the starting point.

Pescadero Creek

BUTANO STATE PARK

Butano State Park was created in 1969 to accommodate the overflow from older, developed state parks such as Big Basin and Portola. Tucked away in a ravine on the ocean-facing slopes of Butano Ridge, this bit of secluded timberland seems much farther from civilization than the 20 or so air-miles that separate it from the Santa Clara Valley and lower Peninsula. Frequent fogs and heavy rainfall contribute to the lush growth of the forest floor. According to local Indian tradition, Butano was a "gathering place of friendly visits." And, what could be more conducive to peaceful gatherings than Mother Nature's own rainforest cathedral?

Located inland from Highway 1 some 50 miles south of San Francisco and 30 miles north of Santa Cruz, the park is nevertheless a good many road-miles from nearly all points in the Bay Area. From the east, you must drive long stretches of winding road before reaching the coast highway. Take Cloverdale Road south from Pescadero, or Gazos Creek Road (unpaved at the time of this writing) east from Highway 1 to reach the park entrance.

The area was selectively logged in the last century, and many a Methuselah remains. In keeping with the wilderness character of the park, developed facilities are minimal. The small campground includes walk-in, as well as drive-in sites, and a trail camp in a remote corner of the park caters to backpackers. Many of the hiking trails more closely resemble deer paths than the wide, heavily-compacted tracks found in the more popular parks. The policy at Butano is to construct and maintain trails to guarantee safe passage, but to avoid bulldozing a path through every obstacle. The trails are uncrowded, typically, and it's possible to spend an entire day in the outlying regions without seeing another person.

Little Butano Creek Trail

Approximate distance: 1.0 mile (1 way)
Low point (trailhead): 300 feet
High point (Pumphouse): 500 feet

From the point at which the trail leaves the paved entrance road (midway between the park office and campground) to the pumphouse a mile away, it winds back and forth several times over Little Butano Creek. Permanent bridges once crossed the little stream, but a flood several years back took away most of them. Flood damage and down wood is confined mostly to the upper end of the trail, but even this part is passable in dry weather now. The upper end joins a service road connecting the pumphouse and a small dam along the creek to the paved road at the campground downstream. You can follow this road back for a different view if you like, or return the same way you came.

Footbridge over Little Butano Creek

42

Little Butano Creek Trail

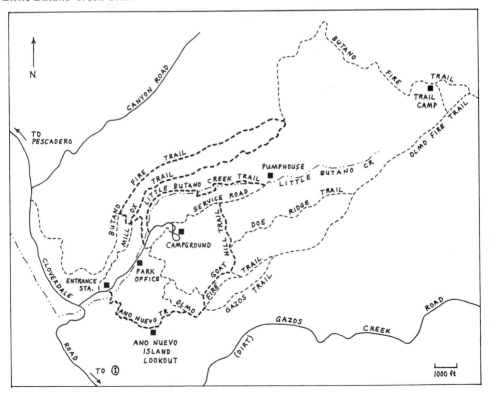

Mill Ox Trail — Butano Fire Trail

Approximate distance: 4.0 miles round trip
Low point (trailhead): 280 feet
High point (Butano Fire Trail): 1,140 feet

To walk on the slopes above Little Butano Creek is to experience the primeval forest as it has existed for thousands of years in the Santa Cruz Mountains. You'll begin this hike among thick stands of redwood and velvety undergrowth of ferns and sorrel along the creek, then ascend through drier mixed forests dominated by craggy Douglas fir to a fire trail overlooking the forest bowl.

A spur trail to Mill Ox Trail, which begins with a footbridge over the creek, intersects the paved road between the park office and the campground. After an initial climb of about one-fourth mile on this trail, you will come to a yellow-topped post. Take the path to the right. The climbing is gradual now as the trail skirts the edge of a clearing. Even in a dry year, water oozes from seeps and springs to nourish the meadow grass here. Finally the trail breaks out of the trees and follows the eroded remains of a dirt road to Butano Fire Trail at the top of the ridge. Cooling ocean breezes sweep in from the west, and on a clear day the dry, pine-covered ridge to the northeast stands bold against an azure sky.

From this high point of the hike, turn west on Butano Fire Trail for a short return to the starting point. Views unfold at every turn, and the gentle downgrade makes the remaining distance seem almost trivial. Don't miss the wooden post indicating Mill Ox Trail on the left. From here there remains a half-mile descent to the creek.

Ano Nuevo Trail — Goat Hill Trail

Approximate distance: 1.0 mile to Ano
Nuevo Lookout
3.0 miles round trip
Low point (trailhead): 215 feet
High point (Lookout): 1,000 feet

The lookout point offering a "panoramic view of Ano Nuevo Island" falls somewhat short of the description noted in the park brochure. More impressive however are the views of rolling meadows, forested ridges, and the coastline as seen from other parts of Ano Nuevo Trail.

You begin at the post indicating Ano Nuevo Trail opposite the entrance station, and plunge immediately into a thicket of blackberry vines that in places nearly close overhead. The trail begins a relentless ascent with tight switchbacks, and the scenery changes to windswept Douglas fir festooned with the parasitic Spanish moss. The picnic table at Ano Nuevo Lookout, at the top of the hill, is a pleasant place to relax. Ano Nuevo (New Year's) Point in the distance was named by explorer Sebastian Vizcaino in January of 1603. Ano Nuevo Island, a half-mile beyond the point, is a favored winter breeding ground of the elephant seal.

An interesting and not so steep return may be made via Goat Hill Trail. Ano Nuevo Trail continues eastward a short half-mile to Olmo Fire Trail. Walk a few hundred feet east on the fire road, and go left when you reach the post designating Goat Hill Trail. Go right at the first trail intersection marked by a yellow-topped stake, then left at the next intersection. Goat Hill Trail continues around the edge of a large open meadow, and finally descends through redwood and Douglas fir to the unpaved service road a quarter-mile above the campground.

Hydrangea

Pump house and dam — Little Butano Creek

HENRY COWELL REDWOODS STATE PARK

Fall Creek Area

Approximate distances: 1.0 mile to Lime Kiln site
3.0 miles round trip
Elevation at trailhead: 500 feet
Low point: 400 feet
High point: 900 feet

Protection of the coast redwoods in what is now Henry Cowell Redwoods State Park began as early as the 1860's, when parts of an original Mexican land grant, Rancho Canada del Rincon, were purchased by Joseph Welsh and Henry Cowell, Sr. Both men sought to preserve the area known as the Big Trees grove — now called the Redwood Grove. In 1930 this grove was acquired by Santa Cruz County for use as a local park. Later, in 1954, it was combined with more than 1500 additional acres gift-deeded to the State of California. A new natural area, the Fall Creek sub-unit on Ben Lomond Mountain, was donated to the state by the Cowell Foundation in 1972.

The main (day-use) entrance to the park is located on Highway 9, one-half mile south of Felton. Facilities here include a large picnic area overlooking the San Lorenzo River from its east bank, and a concession area (gift shop) adjacent to the Redwood Grove. Fifteen miles of riding and hiking trails run throughout the semi-wilderness area south and east of Redwood Grove. Overnighters stay in the 51-unit Graham Hill Campground, located off Graham Hill Road on the eastern edge of the park.

Heard periodically in the Redwood Grove is the shrill whistle announcing the arrival or departure of the Roaring Camp & Big Trees Railroad. This popular tourist attraction adjacent to the park features an original steam-powered narrow-gauge passenger train. Enroute to the summit of Bear Mountain, the train negotiates the steepest railroad grades in North America. Roaring Camp is located on Graham Hill Road, one mile from Felton.

Lush redwood forests and delightful streamside trails aren't the only attractions in the new Fall Creek unit of Henry Cowell State Park. The relics of a once-booming limestone industry may also be seen here. Many of today's park trails, in fact, follow the old logging and wagon supply roads which lead directly to historical sites such as the Barrel Mill and Limestone Kilns.

The 1870's marked the beginning of limestone operations here. Years later the industry produced as much as 30 percent of the lime used in California, and supplied much of the raw material used to rebuild San Francisco after the devastating 1906 earthquake. During this same period, the timber resources of the area were utilized in the construction of barrels to store and transport lime and as fuel to fire the lime kilns. By the 1920's, the limestone and logging industries had moved on, leaving time and the elements to heal the scars and return the works of man to a natural state.

This easy three-mile hike in the Fall Creek area begins at a small dirt parking lot located on Felton-Empire Road, just 0.7 mile west (uphill) of the traffic signal in Felton. From the corner of the parking lot, follow Bennett Creek Trail downhill to Fall Creek and the North Fork Trail. Proceed uphill on North Fork Trail along the left bank of the creek. Within a half-mile you'll reach the South Fork — a small, but vigorous streamlet tumbling out of the ravine on the left. Leave North Fork Trail at this point and begin climbing up the ravine toward the Limestone Kilns about one-quarter mile away. Here you will find a row of kilns, a large rock dump and a neatly-stacked wood pile, all reasonably intact after 60 years of disuse. Other structures in the area have not fared so well.

When you have satisfied yourself with

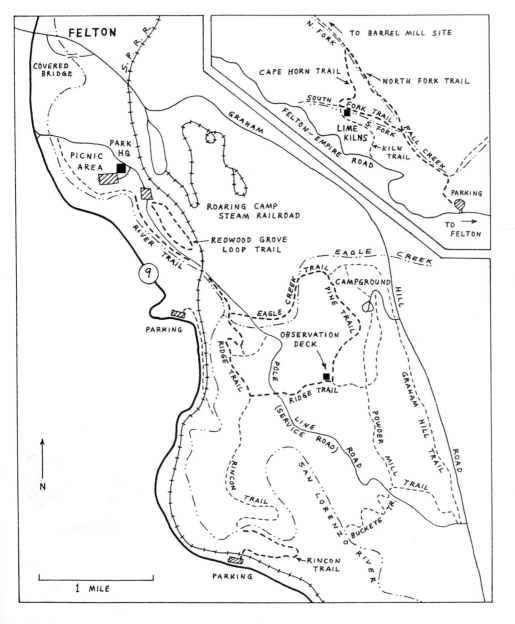

FELTON

COVERED BRIDGE

S.P.R.R.

PARK HQ

PICNIC AREA

GRAHAM

TO BARREL MILL SITE

N. FORK

CAPE HORN TRAIL

NORTH FORK TRAIL

SOUTH FORK TRAIL

FELTON-EMPIRE ROAD

S. FORK

LIME KILNS

KILN TRAIL

FALL CREEK

PARKING

TO FELTON

RIVER TRAIL

9

ROARING CAMP STEAM RAILROAD

REDWOOD GROVE LOOP TRAIL

EAGLE CREEK

EAGLE CREEK TRAIL

PINE TRAIL

CAMPGROUND

EAGLE CREEK TRAIL

PARKING

RIDGE TRAIL

OBSERVATION DECK

POLE LINE (SERVICE ROAD) ROAD

RIDGE TRAIL

GRAHAM HILL TRAIL

POWDER MILL TRAIL

GRAHAM HILL ROAD

RINCON TRAIL

SAN LORENZO RIVER

BUCKEYE TR.

N

1 MILE

PARKING

RINCON TRAIL

47

this fascinating bit of historical evidence, you may continue northward on Cape Horn Trail, contouring along the ridge dividing the North and South Forks. When you reach North Fork, turn and follow the creek downstream for a very pleasant mile. Bennett Creek Trail will return you to the starting point.

Redwood Grove Trail

Approximate distance: 0.8 mile round trip
Trail elevation: 250 feet

The "Big Trees" at Henry Cowell Redwoods State Park look much the same as they did nearly a century ago when railroad passengers enroute to Santa Cruz from San Jose disembarked here for lunch. Now, as then, visitors enjoy the majestic beauty and cathedral-like silence of this primeval redwood forest. An interpretive leaflet is available at park headquarters for the self-guided loop trail that winds among the most distinctive members of the grove.

You'll be walking along a flat terrace overlooking the San Lorenzo River, one of many such terraces cut in the canyon bottom through the ages. Here, beyond reach of winter floods yet close enough to the life-giving moisture it needs, the sequoia finds a comfortable habitat. A few of the trees have commemorative names associated with them. One of the largest is dedicated to Theodore Roosevelt, who stopped by to admire the grove in 1903. The tallest tree presently stands at 285 feet, in spite of the loss of a 75-foot top piece torn off several years ago in a windstorm. Its former height would surely rival today's record-holders in Redwood National Park.

Photographers will enjoy the delicate interplay of light and shadow in Redwood Grove as the sun filters through the forest canopy. During times of cloud cover or low sun angle, however, a tripod may be necessary to accommodate the long exposure times required.

Fire ravaged redwood stump

48

Tanoak forest – Rincon Trail

Redwood Grove to Santa Cruz View

Approximate distances: 2.0 miles to Observation Deck
    4.0 miles round trip
Low point (trailhead): 250 feet
High point (Observation Deck): 810 feet

A cross-section of the varied life zones that exist within Henry Cowell Park may be viewed on this hike from Redwood Grove to the observation deck situated atop an 800-foot knoll in the middle of the park. You may also experience surprising variations of climate, especially on sunny days. On clear winter mornings, in fact, it is not unusual to leave a lingering frost along the banks of the river, only to find shirt-sleeve weather prevailing on the ridge-tops just minutes away.

The four-mile loop described herein begins near the entrance to the Redwood Grove Trail. Follow River Trail downstream along the east bank of the San Lorenzo River. One-third mile beyond the Southern Pacific railroad trestle, take Eagle Creek Trail to the left, climbing steeply alongside the creek. Crossing Eagle Creek, you abruptly enter the environment that differs so markedly from the redwood forest below. Oak, madrone, manzanita and other chaparral vegetation thrive in the sandy soil and sunshine. Stay to the right, following Pine Trail uphill toward the top of the ridge. The most unusual feature of the park is here — a stand of ponderosa pine. Native ponderosa exist in only one other locality in the Santa Cruz Mountains; however, they are common to drier inland areas such as the middle elevations of the Sierra Nevada.

Pine Trail ends at the observation platform, which was constructed on the roof of a concrete water storage tank. Pause here to take in the view of Santa Cruz coastline. Relax in the shade of the nearby ponderosa pine trees.

The gravity-assisted return trip to Redwood Grove via Ridge Trail will probably take less time than you think. Near the confluence of Eagle Creek and San Lorenzo River, Ridge Trail joins River Trail. Continue on River Trail back to the starting point.

Rincon Trail

Approximate distance: 0.5 mile to river
Low point (San Lorenzo River): 100 feet
High point (trailhead): 320 feet

The Rincon Trail provides an easy way to reach a fairly isolated stretch of the San Lorenzo River. It begins at a roadside pullout along Highway 9 about halfway between Felton and Santa Cruz. This is three miles south of the main entrance to the park near Felton.

At the bottom of the trail you may trace the remains of an old redwood flume along the west bank of the river. The San Lorenzo is a placid stream most of the year, bubbling lazily over beds of rock, or spreading out in quiet, mirror-like pools. Legions of fishermen descend upon the river in the high-water months of December through February, when the steelhead, a sea-running rainbow trout, swim upstream to spawn in the protected headwaters of the river. Unlike its sea-going cousins, the salmon, who return only once to the spawning ground, steelhead go back to the ocean after spawning.

Grass hummocks — San Lorenzo River

50

San Lorenzo River

CASTLE ROCK STATE PARK

Castle Rock State Park lies atop the summit ridge dividing Santa Clara County from Santa Cruz County at a point which is probably the most spectacular locale in the Santa Cruz Mountains. To rock climbers who flock here, it is a much sought after wonderland of weirdly-eroded sandstone outcroppings. To others it means a place of quiet beauty to bring the family for a Sunday afternoon outing. But for everyone it provides an opportunity to let the spirit soar free in the great open spaces high above the canyons.

Castle Rock is frequently dusted by snowfall in winter, an event that brings hordes of flatlanders from the cities below. Warmer seasons bring sparkling-clear days when one can watch in a detached sort of way the approaching and receding of the nocturnal summer fogs so familiar to residents of the coast.

Hiking and backpacking are encouraged at Castle Rock State Park, with automobile access limited to parking areas on the periphery. Currently the park consists of about 1,400 acres on the slopes west of Skyline Boulevard, but an eventual 2,500 acres are envisioned when funds become available to purchase additional land.

A big breakthrough in a truly regional concept for the public parks of the Santa Cruz Mountains took place in 1969 with the construction of a 25-mile trail linking Castle Rock to the trail system of Big Basin Redwoods State Park. The completion of this major link in the "Skyline to the Sea Trail" made it possible to walk off-pavement all the way to Highway 1 on the coast. Trail camps have been established at convenient intervals along the way, including one at the park headquarters area of Castle Rock State Park. A map and guide for the Skyline to the Sea Trail is published by the Santa Cruz Mountain Trail Association. See page 77.

Rappelling – Goat Rock

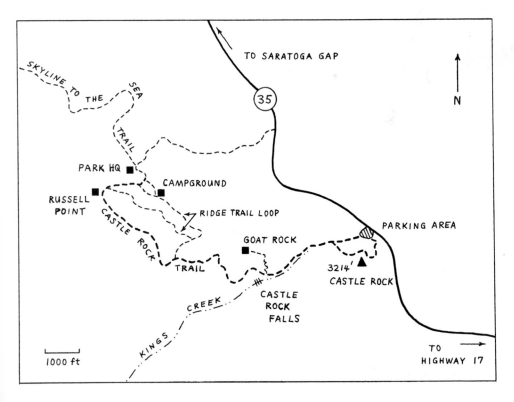

TO SARATOGA GAP

SKYLINE TO THE SEA TRAIL

35

N

PARK HQ

CAMPGROUND

RUSSELL POINT

CASTLE ROCK TRAIL

RIDGE TRAIL LOOP

GOAT ROCK

PARKING AREA

3214'
CASTLE ROCK

KINGS CREEK

CASTLE ROCK FALLS

1000 ft

TO HIGHWAY 17

Castle Rock Trail

Approximate distances: 0.3 mile (1 way) to Castle Rock
    1.0 mile (1 way) to Castle Rock Falls
    3.0 miles (1 way) to park headquarters
Elevation at trailhead: 3,020 ft.
Low point (near park headquarters): 2,380 feet
High point (Castle Rock): 3,214 feet

Unlike many trails in this book, this one *ends,* not begins, at park headquarters. To reach the starting point, drive to the large parking area off Skyline Boulevard (Highway 35), just 2½ miles south of the junction of Highways 9 and 35 at Saratoga Gap. It is advisable to bring water along, particularly on summer days.

An alternate trail to Castle Rock begins on the opposite side of the parking lot from Skyline Boulevard and starts climbing immediately through tanoak and Douglas fir. Regardless of the hour, you're sure to come upon at least one group of climbers at the pock-marked 80-foot high lump of sandstone that is the namesake of the park. A multitude of handholds and footholds on the surface of the rock make it a perfect training ground for novices at the art.

After looping back downhill to the bottom of a deeply shaded ravine, turn left onto the main trail. Intersecting the main trail from the right is an "unofficial" trail that heads steeply uphill to Goat Rock, again a popular spot for climbing. Kings Creek originates from springs in the ravine and runs peacefully along until it experiences an abrupt 100-foot plunge at Castle Rock Falls. An observation platform built along the trail offers a good view of not only the falls, but also the entire canyon through which Kings Creek flows to join the San Lorenzo River.

The trail then continues two miles on a gradually descending gradient to park headquarters. This section bears little resemblance to the first part of the trip. Shaded belts of oak, bay and madrone alternate with a dense ground cover of low-growing chaparral. Some of the slopes get downright precipitous, but provide awe-inspiring views of the unbroken carpet of evergreen forest that extends out to Big Basin and flat-topped Ben Lomond Mountain. If you're a photography buff, it's a sin to forget your camera. The mountains of Monterey Peninsula can usually be seen on the far side of Monterey Bay. Look for the white fringe of sand along the base of the Peninsula on fog-free days.

At park headquarters you can refill canteens and relax in one of the picnic sites. A nature trail guide is available at the office for those who wish to learn more about three biotic communities — the mixed evergreen community, the streamside community, and the chaparral community — in the vicinity of the campground.

54

Castle Rock

BIG BASIN
REDWOODS STATE PARK

In May, 1900, a group of distinguished citizens interested in saving the redwoods set out to explore and report upon the Big Basin area as a possible site for a public park. Their journey on foot across a trackless wilderness of sun-dappled ridges and swift-flowing streams was an impressive prelude to the wonders that would lie ahead in the deep redwood forest of the basin itself. Andrew P. Hill, leader of the group, writes of their discovery of the first truly gigantic tree:

> "As we emerged into the opening before this tree, I noticed members of our party looking at this giant with open mouths, and suddenly I became aware of being in the same condition! Our awe increased as we further explored this wonderful forest."

The Sempervirens Club, an organization formed almost on the spot by members of this expedition, took responsibility for bringing into public attention the issue of preserving the redwoods for future generations. Two years later their efforts resulted in the establishment of a 3,800-acre "California Redwood Park," the forerunner of the more than 200 units in the California park system today. Were it not for the timely actions of these concerned individuals, large stands of virgin redwood in the Santa Cruz Mountains would now be nonexistent. In the critical period after 1900, these remaining groves were directly in the path of loggers advancing up the canyons in search of old-growth timber for their steam-powered sawmills.

The park was later renamed Big Basin Redwoods State Park, and its boundaries expanded to include a present total of over 12,000 acres. Considerable development of the inner park has taken place over the years to accommodate its half-million or so annual visitors. In spite of the crush, it's possible to find solitude — even on busy days — by hiking a good distance away from the main area. Some trails follow the creeks; others climb to scenic vista points overlooking the forest canopy of the basin and the rugged

Pacific coastline. All trails are well-marked and easy to follow.

Motorists may approach Big Basin from either end of the access road (Highway 236) that loops through the park. One end joins Highway 9 at Waterman Gap, 8 miles northwest of park headquarters. This narrow and twisting route is the most convenient for Bay Area people, but it should not be used by vehicles with campers or trailers. The main road out of the park, which is wide enough for any type of vehicle, runs 10 miles southeast to Highway 9 at Boulder Creek.

The usual facilities of a fully developed park are here at Big Basin: 190 individual family campsites, 158 picnic sites, two large group camp areas — even a snack bar and gift shop. To familiarize yourself with the natural history of the region, visit the Nature Lodge in the main area of the park. Of particular interest to the hiker is the large-scale relief map of the basin showing vegetation types and hiking trails. Also on exhibit are some of Andrew P. Hill's 1900's photographs of the redwoods.

In the following descriptions of Big Basin trails, all walks begin in the main area around park headquarters.

Columbian black tailed deer

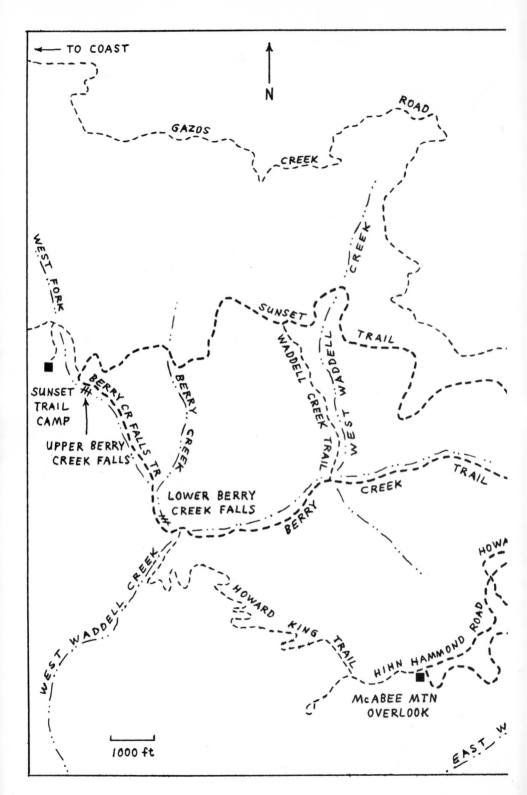

TO COAST

N

GAZOS CREEK ROAD

WEST FORK

SUNSET TRAIL CAMP

UPPER BERRY CREEK FALLS

BERRY CR FALLS TR

BERRY CREEK

SUNSET

WADDELL CREEK

WEST WADDELL

CREEK

TRAIL

WEST WADDELL CREEK TRAIL

LOWER BERRY CREEK FALLS

BERRY CREEK TRAIL

WEST WADDELL CREEK

HOWARD KING TRAIL

HIHN HAMMOND ROAD

HOWA

McABEE MTN OVERLOOK

EAST W

1000 ft

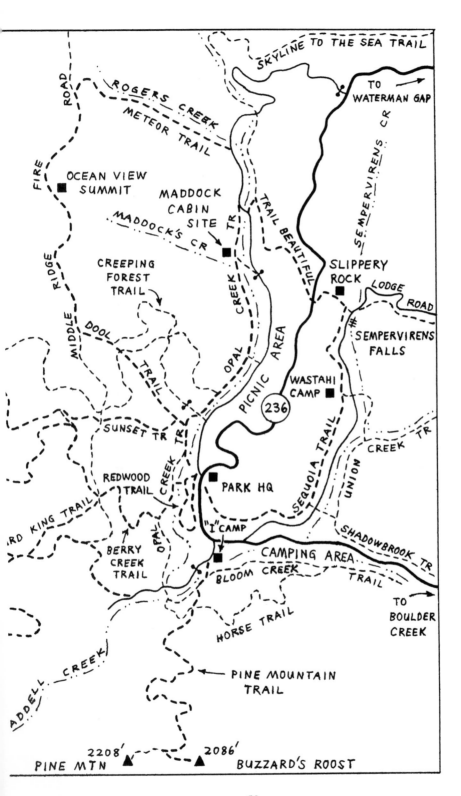

SKYLINE TO THE SEA TRAIL

TO WATERMAN GAP

ROGERS CREEK

METEOR TRAIL

FIRE ROAD

SEMPERVIRENS CR.

OCEAN VIEW SUMMIT

MADDOCK CABIN SITE

MADDOCK'S CR.

CREEK TR.

TRAIL BEAUTIFUL

SLIPPERY ROCK

CREEPING FOREST TRAIL

MIDDLE RIDGE

DOOL TRAIL

OPAL CREEK

LODGE ROAD

SEMPERVIRENS FALLS

PICNIC AREA

SUNSET TR.

CREEK TR.

236

WASTAHI CAMP

SEQUOIA TRAIL

UNION CREEK

CREEK TR.

REDWOOD TRAIL

RD KING TRAIL

OPAL

PARK HQ

"I" CAMP

BERRY CREEK TRAIL

SHADOWBROOK TR.

CAMPING AREA

BLOOM CREEK

TRAIL

TO BOULDER CREEK

HORSE TRAIL

ADDELL CREEK

PINE MOUNTAIN TRAIL

2208' PINE MTN   2086' BUZZARD'S ROOST

Redwood Trail

Approximate distance: 0.6 mile round trip
Trail elevation: 960 feet

This famous trail has been walked by several million people since Big Basin was declared a state park in 1902. Before embarking, pick up a copy of the "Redwood Trail Guide" at park headquarters.

The majority of the best known and individually named trees in the park are along this trail. Fire scars have created a remarkable. variety of forms. The list includes the 17-foot diameter "Santa Clara Tree," the near-perfect "Daughter Tree," the 2,000-year old "Father of the Forest," and the 329-foot tall "Mother of the Forest."

Ocean View Summit – Meteor Trail

Approximate distances: 2.0 miles to Ocean
  View Summit
  5.0 miles round trip
Low point (park headquarters): 1,000 feet
High point (Middle Ridge): 1,760 feet

Rising nearly 700 feet to Ocean View Summit, this loop includes a little of everything characteristic of the Big Basin region — from streamside old-growth redwoods to wispy stands of knobcone pine and barren sandstone on the summit.

Begin by crossing Opal Creek on the footbridge west of the Nature Lodge at the park headquarters. Follow Opal Creek Trail north to Dool Trail. A moderate uphill climb on Dool Trail brings you to Middle Ridge Fire Road. This ridge was used by Costanoan Indians as a crossing through the area. They preferred open country where game was plentiful, and avoided the dark redwood forest on their journeys over the mountains between settlements in the Santa Clara Valley and intermittently used campsites along the coast. Perhaps these early inhabitants regarded the deep woods with religious superstition; certainly the presence of grizzly bears was a deterrent.

Near the high point of Middle Ridge, a panoramic view of the ocean opens up — here's a good spot for a picnic lunch. The exposed sandstone on the summit is part of the Butano Formation, which underlies the region to great depths. A half-mile north of Ocean View Summit is Meteor Trail, the half-way point on this hike. The remainder is entirely downhill following streambeds. Along Rogers Creek you'll pass through the typical mixed forest of redwood, Douglas fir, tanoak and madrone. The creekbed is covered by a carpet of ferns and moss, and a variety of shade-loving flowering plants take shelter under the forest canopy.

Turn right on the paved road at the foot of Meteor Trail, then follow the blacktop south to Opal Creek Trail, which begins as a parallel path on the right. The road soon crosses the creek and disappears from view. Opal Creek Trail is flanked by tall redwoods on both sides, and you are rarely out of sight of the creek. The opalescent color of the water, incidentally, is due to plant-mineral action, not pollution.

Nothing is left of the cabin built on the bank of Opal Creek by homesteader Tom Maddock in 1883; only a sign indicating its location along the trail. Maddock earned his living here by harvesting tanbark for the leather industry of the Santa Clara Valley. The cabin, which was built of boards split from a single tree using only simple tools, was destroyed in the 1950's.

Sequoia Trail – Trail Beautiful

Approximate distances: 1.7 miles to Semper-
  virens Falls
  4.3 miles round trip
Low point (park headquarters): 1,000 feet
High point: 1,360 feet

This route is most rewarding in the off-season, non-summer months for two reasons. First, the trail never strays far from paved roads, camping or picnic areas, and these can get downright congested at times. Second, the Slippery Rock area, which is so delightfully green and moist in the winter, is bone dry and open to the full glare of the sun in summer.

Sequoia Trail begins at the park headquarters building and follows Lodge Road

Chimney Tree

up through Wastahi walk-in campground. At 1.7 miles walk across the road for a look at Sempervirens Falls. In the early years of the state park, the area around the falls was used as a camp ground by the Sempervirens Club. The Club, in fact, was organized at nearby Slippery Rock in 1900 for the purpose of preserving the redwoods of Big Basin. The "Save the Redwoods" movement can trace its origins back to this event.

The next leg of the trip takes you up the exposed sandstone of Slippery Rock to Highway 236 and Trail Beautiful. The rest is downhill. Observe the fire scars on the larger trees along Trail Beautiful — these were inflicted by the last really big fire in 1904. At the bottom of the hill, you have a choice of completing the loop by either Opal Creek Trail, or the less scenic but slightly more direct paved road through the picnic area.

Pine Mountain Trail

Approximate distance: 2.3 miles (1 way) to Buzzard's Roost
Low point (park headquarters): 1,000 feet
High point (Buzzard's Roost): 2,086 feet

To reach Pine Mountain Trail, walk south from park headquarters along Highway 236. A path is provided on the right side of the road for pedestrians. Enter the "I" camp and proceed to campsite 10, where a trail leaves the road and crosses a footbridge over Bloom Creek. Continue along the bank 0.1 mile, then follow Pine Mountain Trail up the slope.

The ascent to the promontory known as Buzzard's Roost involves an elevation gain of just over a thousand feet, and includes, as do most ridge trails, a remarkable variety of life zones. Forest fires swept Pine Mountain in 1936 and 1948, destroying the vegetation on the upper slopes. Since then a vigorous new growth of knobcone pine, a pale and scrawny tree adapted to dry, rocky terrain, has risen from the ashes. Fire is an essential element in the reproductive cycle of the knobcone. Only a conflagration can release seed from the resin-sealed cones and allow the seed to fall upon a fertile bed of freshly exposed mineral soil.

Topside you'll find sandstone outcroppings amid the pine and chaparral, the most prominent being Buzzard's Roost. True to its name, you should be able to see from here the winged scavengers — actually turkey vultures — in action as they wheel overhead. You will have a good view of the Scott Creek and Waddell Creek drainages, but the ocean is partly hidden behind the summit of Pine Mountain to the west.

McAbee Mountain Overlook

Approximate distance: 2.5 miles (1 way)
Elevation at park headquarters: 1,000 feet
High point (McAbee Mountain Overlook): 1,730 feet

McAbee Mountain may be reached by either foot trail or fire road. I would suggest making the climb on the trails, then returning quickly and easily on the road. Start on Redwood Trail, but follow the signs indicating "Outlying Trails" which appears a short distance out near the restrooms. Cross Opal Creek, walk south (left) on Opal Creek Trail, then go right at Berry Creek Trail to begin the climb. When you reach the five-way intersection of trails on Middle Ridge, continue across to Howard King Trail.

Howard King Trail follows the general route of Hihn Hammond Road, but no effort was made in its construction to smooth out the topography. Up and over, down and around, this trail accommodates the lay of the land. It ends at a clearing on the road that overlooks the East Waddell Creek watershed. You can relax on a log bench and admire the ocean, or rather the fingers of fog that creep inland from the coastal bank. In the canyon below, William Waddell directed an ambitious lumber enterprise beginning about 1862. In addition to a sawmill and other buildings housing the labor force, he constructed a wharf on the seacoast and ran a horse tram up the canyon to the mill. Waddell was fatally mauled by a grizzly bear in 1875. The beehive sawdust burner visible down there today is a relic from a much more recent logging period.

Pine Mountain Trail

For a fast return to park headquarters, take Hihn Hammond Road down to the paved road through the "I" campground. If you prefer to take your time, there are diversions along the way. Listen for the tapping of the acorn woodpecker. With a little patience and binoculars you can watch this fascinating bird go about its chores.

Berry Creek Falls – Sunset Trail Loop

Approximate distances: 4.0 miles to Lower Berry Creek Falls
10.0 miles round trip
Elevation at park headquarters: 1,000 feet
Low point (West Waddell Creek): 350 feet
High point (Middle Ridge): 1,350 feet

I have had a sense of discovery in each of several trips taken to Berry Creek Falls over the years. The first glimpse of the falls through the redwoods never fails to elicit wonder and surprise; perhaps this feeling is heightened by the fact that they are truly remote and accessible only on foot. The 10-mile loop described here is an arduous hike for most people, but one that is well within the capability of anyone in reasonable physical condition, provided enough time is allowed. Five to six hours is sufficient, but take a full day if you intend to browse along the way. In any case, be sure to allow time to return before sunset.

To begin the hike take Redwood Trail, Opal Creek Trail, then Berry Creek Trail to Middle Ridge as in the McAbee Mountain trail description above; but remain on Berry Creek Trail past the summit. Several wooden footbridges built over small ravines by the Civilian Conservation Corps in the 1930's have deteriorated or been washed away during winter storms. These are being gradually replaced or restored through the efforts of a modern-day counterpart of the CCC, the Youth Conservation Corps. The Waddell Creek Trail, intersecting Berry Creek Trail from the right, can be used as a "bail-out" route to short-cut the loop to 7½ miles, but you miss out on the falls as a consequence. Berry Creek Trail continues through the moist environment along the bank of West Waddell Creek. Mosses, ferns and shade-loving shrubs grow in profusion along the trail. Mushrooms are common in the winter and early spring. Where access permits, look along the creekside for newts, salamanders, and the native "banana slugs" that sometimes grow to eight inches in length.

Four miles out, the trail fords the creek, then offers a first view of Lower Berry Creek Falls in the canyon to the right. Coming abreast of the falls, you can admire the feathery cascades and the glistening pool of water lying below. Flanking cliffs covered with dripping moss and five-finger ferns round out this beautiful natural water temple.

Upper Berry Creek Falls, sometimes known as Silver and Golden Falls, are a mile upstream from the lower falls. The water tumbles carefree over a series of sandstone terraces and abrupt cliffs. A metal cable guides those unsure of step over some slippery terraces near the top of the falls.

Though somewhat anticlimatic, the return on Sunset Trail includes an inside view of some of the best virgin groves in the park. Winding up and down the hillsides among the headwaters of Berry Creek and West Waddell Creek, the trail attains a final summit at Middle Ridge. From here it's an easy downhill jaunt back to Opal Creek Trail.

Buzzard's Roost

FOREST OF NISENE MARKS STATE PARK

Nature Trail

Approximate distance: 9.5 miles (1 way) between locked gates
Elevation at upper locked gate: 2,440 feet
Low point (lower locked gate): 325 feet
High point (Santa Rosalia Ridge): 2,575 feet

With a little help from a friend, the dirt road known as the "Nature Trail" through the heart of the Forest can be leisurely travelled on foot in the space of a half-day. Simply have your friend transport you to the locked gate in the upper end of the park, then return, after a few hours at the beach perhaps, to pick you up below the locked gate in the lower end of the park.

One of the best-kept secrets of the Santa Cruz Mountains is the existence of this 10,000-acre semi-wilderness preserve just a few miles up-canyon from the beach community of Aptos, near Santa Cruz. The lack of advertising is appropriate since there are few facilities here to accommodate visitors. The Forest was a gift to the people of California from Herman Marks and his family, and it was their intention that the park remain largely undeveloped. It is a haven for hikers and nature-freaks, quiet and uncrowded.

To reach the lower end of the park, take Highway 1 to the Aptos turnoff, then proceed southeast (away from Santa Cruz) on Soquel Drive. Turn left just beyond the railroad bridge in the middle of town. Neither a street sign, nor any indication of a state park marks this intersection. After crossing the railroad tracks this road becomes Aptos Creek Road, and the familiar small brown-and-yellow state park signs soon appear. There is no park office, but you should find some leaflets clipped to an information board in a small parking area on the left. Two small picnic areas are nearby in dense groves of redwood. Motor vehicles may go as far as the locked gate four miles up from Aptos. Travel on foot only is allowed beyond this point.

The park is used mostly for day hiking, although a trail camp is available for one-night use by backpackers. Reservations for this camp must be made through the office at Henry Cowell Redwoods State Park. Remember to bring a canteen if you intend to stay any length of time in the park, since water is not always available.

Five Finger fern at Aptos Creek

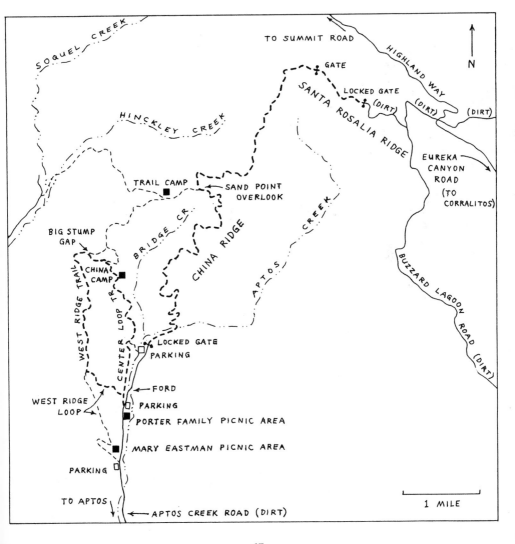

SOQUEL CREEK

TO SUMMIT ROAD

HIGHLAND WAY

N

GATE

LOCKED GATE (DIRT)

(DIRT)

(DIRT)

SANTA ROSALIA RIDGE

HINCKLEY CREEK

EUREKA CANYON ROAD (TO CORRALITOS)

TRAIL CAMP

SAND POINT OVERLOOK

BRIDGE CR.

CHINA RIDGE

APTOS CREEK

BIG STUMP GAP

WEST RIDGE TRAIL

CHINA CAMP

BUZZARD LAGOON ROAD (DIRT)

CENTER LOOP TR.

LOCKED GATE PARKING

FORD

WEST RIDGE LOOP

PARKING

PORTER FAMILY PICNIC AREA

MARY EASTMAN PICNIC AREA

PARKING

1 MILE

TO APTOS

APTOS CREEK ROAD (DIRT)

Finding the trailhead at the top requires some detective work — like the main entrance down below, there are no signs up here either. If you approach by way of Eureka Canyon Road from Corralitos, watch the small mile markers on the right side of the road. Turn left at Buzzard Lagoon Road, which is the first intersecting dirt road after mile 8.75. Go one mile on Buzzard Lagoon Road, then make a sharp right and continue another mile to the locked gate. If approaching from Highway 17 via Summit Road and Highland Way, look behind you at the mileposts on the opposite side of the road. These originate from 0.00 at Buzzard Lagoon Road.

From the high point on the trail of 2,575 feet at Santa Rosalia Ridge, you descend to a low of 325 feet at the locked gate along Aptos Creek. And, since most of the intervening grade is mild, it is surprising how quickly the miles are covered. The vegetation changes from mixed forest dominated by madrone and California bay near the top to second-growth redwood at the bottom. A few ancient fire-scarred giants that were spared the logger's axe can be seen on the upper slopes. Sand Point Overlook, near the half-way point, offers an outstanding view of the Santa Cruz coastline.

Unless you are backpacking, plan to do this hike in the dry season, when roads into the park are in passable condition. One additional comment: you may want to set up your rendezvous with transportation at the parking lot next to the lower gate. However a better choice might be the Porter Family Picnic Area a mile down from the gate. This is not only a nice place to relax after the hike, but more important, it is situated below a ford on Aptos Creek Road that can prove to be a problem for some automobiles.

Center Loop Trail — West Ridge Trail

Approximate distances: 2.0 miles to China Camp
5.0 miles round trip
Elevation at trailhead: 230 feet
High point (West Ridge): 1,100 feet

A long-forgotten logging camp is the highlight of this trip over primitive hiking trails in the Forest of Nisene Marks. Built near the turn of the century and housing up to 300 workers in its heyday, China Camp was located at the terminus of a narrow-gauge steam railway that led out to the mill. You will be walking on parts of the old railroad bed enroute to the camp. The old ties underfoot give mute testimony to the days when 15 million board feet of lumber glided over polished rails to feed the demand of the cities and towns below.

If parking spaces are not found in the turnout opposite the Center Loop trailhead, then backtrack a short distance to the large clearing at Porter Family Picnic Area. The path to China Camp follows the gentle railroad grade, but detours occasionally to avoid bridges that have fallen into the steep ravines. It's easy to be misled by false trails cutting in from all sides — just remember that a railroad grade always avoids extremes. Most of the wooden buildings in the camp have been reduced to piles of rubble, but two large structures remain standing. Please leave the site as you found it — it is on state property and protected because of its historical value.

The return to the starting point by way of West Ridge should only be attempted by experienced hikers. Others should return the way they came. Some slippery, steep slopes must be traversed the West Ridge Trail, and the path is hemmed in, actually overgrown in places, by poison oak. Don't wear shorts if you try this route!

UVAS CANYON PARK

Here's another little-known gem tucked away in the eastern folds of the Santa Cruz Mountains. Uvas Canyon Park, administered by the County of Santa Clara, is located at the head of Uvas Canyon about 25 miles south of San Jose. The big attractions here are the many crystal-clear streams and gentle waterfalls found in all corners of this 580-acre park. Although most creeks are perennial, the water level is highest during and immediately after the winter rains, so a visit from November to May would be most rewarding. Late spring brings the added attraction of the fragrance of blooming plants.

The park is located four miles west of Uvas Road at the terminus of Croy Road. Before reaching the park, the road narrows to one lane and passes among some well-kept cabins and a club house which make up the Swedish colony of Sveadal, founded in the 1920's. Pick up a map and nature trail guide at the ranger's office near the entrance to the park. Drive up the road a little ways to the large dirt lot on the right for day use. Adjoining the parking lot is a shaded picnic area above Swanson Creek Falls. A small campground farther along the road overlooks Uvas Creek and is available first come, first serve.

Uvas Creek Trail

Approximate distance: 0.4 mile (1 way)
Elevation at Uvas Creek: 1,000 feet

Two views of Swanson Creek Falls are featured on this trail: from above, and from below. Beginning behind the picnic area, the trail follows the bank of Uvas Creek to the campground a short distance away. Exercise caution in the descent from the picnic grounds past the falls to Uvas Creek, as the trail becomes narrow with a dangerous drop-off to one side. In dry years scarcely a trickle may pass over the falls; at other times a torrent rushes over the edge and plunges 25 feet to join Uvas Creek. Uvas itself is more dependable. Arising from springs on the slopes of Loma Prieta, the highest point of the Santa Cruz Mountains, it flows steadily in any season.

Swanson Creek Trail

Approximate distance: 0.8 mile (1 way) to Old Hot House Site
Low point (trailhead): 1,100 feet
High point: 1,640 feet

This trail begins on the edge of the paved road entering the campground. The elevation gain is about 500 feet through Swanson Canyon, with a rest area about half-way up. Numbered posts alongside the first part of the trail correspond to descriptions of trees and shrubs in the interpretive leaflet available at the ranger's office. In addition to several riffles and falls along Swanson Creek, short hikes up two of the side canyons will reveal Black Rock Falls and Basin Falls. These tributaries are dry in summer.

Near the end of Swanson Creek Trail you will find the remains of a hot water system used to warm an early settler's greenhouse. In cold weather, water was drawn from the creek, heated by fire underneath the maze of pipes you see here, and circulated throughout the building. Another remnant of this homestead is an olive orchard that still survives on the upper slopes of the canyon.

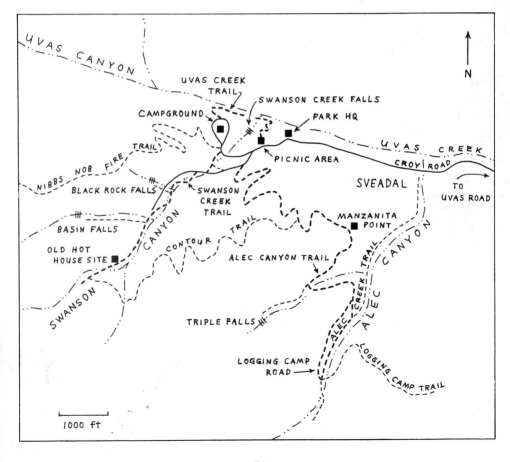

UVAS CANYON

UVAS CREEK TRAIL

SWANSON CREEK FALLS

CAMPGROUND

PARK HQ

UVAS CREEK

CROY ROAD

NIBBS NOB FIRE TRAIL

PICNIC AREA

SVEADAL

TO UVAS ROAD

BLACK ROCK FALLS

SWANSON CREEK TRAIL

MANZANITA POINT

BASIN FALLS

CONTOUR TRAIL

OLD HOT HOUSE SITE

SWANSON

CANYON

ALEC CANYON TRAIL

ALEC CREEK TRAIL

ALEC CANYON

TRIPLE FALLS

LOGGING CAMP ROAD

LOGGING CAMP TRAIL

N

1000 ft

Alec Canyon Trail

Approximate distances: 1.0 mile (1 way) to Manzanita Point
2.0 miles (1 way) to Alec Canyon
Low point (trailhead): 1,080 feet
High point (Manzanita Point): 1,510 feet

Alec Canyon is a place to go for solitude. Here, in a steep ravine deeply shaded by redwoods, you will find the opportunity to listen to the sound of water trickling over boulders; to think, meditate, relax, and simply forget all earthly cares.

To get there take Alec Canyon Trail — actually a fire road — uphill to Manzanita Point. From this vantage point overlooking Uvas Canyon, you can see clear out to the Diablo Range on the other side of the Santa Clara Valley. Notice that the relative scarcity of rain east of here has resulted in oak-studded grassland, a vegetative cover more suited to arid conditions. Also look for the unique stand of tall conifers on the highest ridge in the distance. This is Pine Ridge, a part of Henry Coe State Park.

Beyond Manzanita Point, the trail snakes downhill along sunscorched slopes toward Alec Canyon. The temperature drops perceptibly as you come to the sign indicating Alec Creek Trail, a small footpath on the left. Take this down to the delightful little stream at the bottom.

Follow Alec Creek upstream to the footbridge. The site of an old logging camp is nearby. The few redwoods and Douglas firs that remained after logging activity in the late 19th century were destroyed by fires in the early 20th century. New growth has all but erased the scars; even so the charred remains of many stumps are still very much in evidence here.

For a quick return to civilization, follow the "Logging Camp Road" back to Alec Canyon Trail. And, if time permits, pay a visit to Triple Falls which is a quarter mile off the main trail. You can take Contour Trail, a 1½ mile link to the upper end of Swanson Creek Trail, if you feel obliged to dissipate some more energy.

Swanson Creek

MOUNT MADONNA PARK

In 1927, Santa Clara County purchased the 3,096 acres contained in this park from the estate of cattle baron Henry Miller. Miller had constructed a summer headquarters for himself and two cottages for members of his family at what would become known as Mount Madonna. He chose this particular spot in the Santa Cruz Mountains because of its equable summer climate and its proximity to some of his most important business operations. After the death in 1887 of his partner, Mr. Lux, Miller gained full control of a million acres of land in California, Oregon and Nevada, with no less than one million cattle. The vast empire collapsed after Miller's death in 1916, and only ruins remain today of his summer home. But the surrounding property has seen extensive development as a delightful county park.

Mount Madonna Park is easily reached by Hecker Pass Road (Highway 152) from Gilroy or Watsonville. You can also use the back entrance on Mount Madonna Road. Park headquarters and the nearby Miller summer home site are just off Pole Line Road, about two miles from the main entrance at the summit of Highway 152. Picnic areas and campgrounds available on a first come, first serve basis are sprinkled liberally throughout the park, and a complete network of hiking and bridle trails criss-crosses the mountain. Plant communities ranging from redwood forest to meadow and chaparral are here, and the terrain varies from flat tableland at the summit of Mount Madonna (elevation 1,897 feet) to precipitous canyon slopes.

Sprig Lake Trail — Giant Twins Trail

Approximate distance: 4.0 miles round trip
Low point (trailhead): 480 feet
High point: 1,580 feet

The majority of the 18 miles of trail at Mount Madonna consists of fire roads and bridle paths. Hiking and horseback riding are compatible uses for these trails, of course, but most hikers prefer the quiet and intimacy of a narrow footpath to a dusty road. The most interesting, though certainly not the easiest of the foot trails, begins at Sprig Lake on the lower elevation eastern edge of the park. A loop through the redwood forest with a look at the Giant Twins, and a visit to the Valley View overlook are highlights of this route.

You'll find Sprig Lake, a children's fishing pond and picnic area, on Highway 152 at mile marker 3.00 (three miles east of the main entrance). Sprig Lake Trail is known locally as a "weightwatcher's trail," a good one to work off extra pounds and tone up leg muscles. Those who do not consider it a challenge are invited to carry weights in their pockets! In warm weather be sure to take along a filled canteen. A few gulps of cold water and a generous splash in the face might just provide the motivation you need to continue climbing.

A little more than a mile above Sprig Lake, the trail levels and passes behind a camping area. When you enter a sunny patch of chaparral, mostly manzanita, take the trail to the left that leads to Valley View Road. Cross the road and continue through the redwood groves to the Giant Twins, two gnarled partriarchs sharing a common root system. The remains of an enormous shell enclosing these trees indicates there were probably other family members living here in the past.

From the Giant Twins, walk up the paved road to the parking area overlooking the southern Santa Clara Valley and Diablo Range. Nearby, an old fire road, later turning into a small trail, leads down to join Sprig Lake Trail for the return to the starting point.

Giant Twins

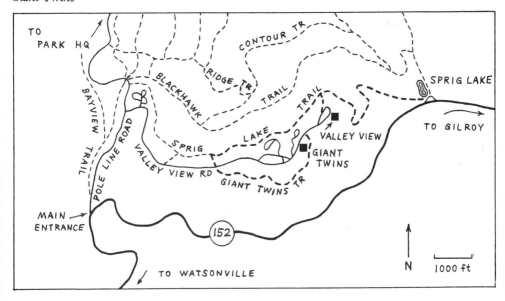

APPENDIX

SANTA CRUZ MOUNTAIN PARKS

Huddart Park (page 32)
1100 Kings Mountain Road
Woodside, CA 94062
(415) 851-0326

Sam McDonald Park (page 34)
(415) 747-0403

or contact
Parks and Recreation Commission
San Mateo County Government Center
Redwood City, CA 94063
(415) 364-5600, ext 2393

Pescadero Creek Park (page 34)
For information contact ranger at Sam
McDonald Park, or contact —
Parks and Recreation Commission
San Mateo County Government Center
Redwood City, CA 94063
(415) 364-5600, ext 2393

San Mateo County Memorial Park (page 36)
9500 Pescadero Road
La Honda, CA 94020
(415) 879-0212

Portola State Park (page 38)
Star Route 2
La Honda, CA 94020
(415) 948-9098

Butano State Park (page 42)
P.O. Box 9
Pescadero, CA 94060
(415) 879-0173

Henry Cowell Redwoods State Park (page 46)
P.O. Box P-1
Felton, CA 95018
(408) 335-4598

Castle Rock State Park (page 52)
15000 Skyline Boulevard
Los Gatos, CA 95030
(408) 867-2952

Big Basin Redwoods State Park (page 56)
Big Basin, CA 95006
(408) 338-6132

Forest of Nisene Marks State Park (page 66)
for information contact
Henry Cowell Redwoods State Park
P.O. Box P-1
Felton, CA 95018
(408) 335-4598

Uvas Canyon Park (page 70)
for information contact
Santa Clara County Parks and Recreation
Department
70 West Hedding Street
San Jose, CA 95110
(408) 356-7151

Mount Madonna Park (page 74)
for information contact
Santa Clara County Parks and Recreation
Department
70 West Hedding Street
San Jose, CA 95110
(408) 356-7151

For additional information on the Santa
Cruz Mountain's write to:

Santa Cruz Mountains Natural History As-
sociation
P.O. Box P-1
Felton, CA 95018

Santa Cruz Mountain Trail Association /
Sempervirens Fund
P.O. Box 1141
Los Altos, CA 94022

Author Jerry Schad

James Simoni

ABOUT THE AUTHOR

Jerry Schad is a fourth-generation descendant of early Santa Clara Valley pioneer Pierre Pellier. Born and raised in San Jose, he has explored the Santa Cruz Mountains extensively by car, bicycle and on foot. Currently living in San Diego, he continues to make frequent visits to Northern California. His other books include *50 Southern California Bicycle Trips* (with coauthor Don Krupp) and *Backcountry Roads & Trails, San Diego County*, both published by The Touchstone Press.

**Cover photo: Lower Berry Creek Falls — Big
Basin Redwoods State Park**

Thomas K. Worcester